Rosemary Palmeira was born in Portugal and now lives in Kingston-upon-Thames. She has had numerous poems published in poetry magazines and anthologies, including *Transformation* (ed. J. Ramsay, Rivelin Grapheme, 1988) and she performs occasionally. She is currently working on her own collection, and on translations of contemporary Portuguese poetry. She is married, with two young children.

Rosemary Palmeira: *Editor*

IN THE GOLD
OF FLESH

Poems of Birth and Motherhood

THE WOMEN'S PRESS

First published by The Women's Press Limited 1990
A member of the Namara Group
34 Great Sutton Street, London EC1V 0DX

Introduction and collection copyright © Rosemary Palmeira 1990

British Library Cataloguing in Publication Data
In the gold of flesh: poems of birth and motherhood.
  I. Palmeira, Rosemary
  821'.914'08

  ISBN 0-7043-4234-0

Phototypeset by Input Typesetting Ltd, London

Printed and bound in Great Britain by
BPCC Hazell Books
Aylesbury Bucks, England
Member of BPCC Ltd.

This book is dedicated with love
to Elizabeth, Luis and Joel and Juliet
without whom

We are part of the circle. When we paint, when we weave, when we write, when we give birth, when we organise, when we heal, when we run through the park, while the redwoods sweat mist, when we do what we were afraid to do, we are not separate. We are of the world and of each other, and the power within us is a great, if not an invincible, power. Though we can be hurt, we can heal, though each one of us can be destroyed, within us is the power of renewal.

STARHAWK *The Spiral Dance* (Beacon Press)

We know that the whole creation has been groaning in pains of labour together until now; . . . for the creation itself will be set free from its bondage to decay and obtain the glorious liberty of the children of God.

(Romans 8.19, 22, 21)

CONTENTS

Contents

The Way Out is through Fire – **Labour**

Aloud into the Light – **Birth**

Still Soft under your Skin – **Newborn**

Contents

Can't Not Never Do Nothing Right – **Motherhood**

Where the Mesh is Wound – **Letting Go**

Contents

Acknowledgments

The author and publishers wish to thank the following publishers, poets and agents for permission to reprint copyright material:

Alta for 'from Placenta Praevia'; Judith Wright's 'Woman to Man' and 'Woman To Child' reproduced from *Collected Poems* 1942–1970 by kind permission of the publishers, Angus & Robertson, (1971); 'The Woman with Love Child' and 'The Woman with Too Many Children Already' Copyright © 1988 by Laura Chester. Reprinted from *In the Zone: new and selected writing* with the permission of Black Sparrow Press; 'The Heir', 'Transformation', 'The Way Out', 'Creation', 'The Dream', 'The Miracle' and 'Song of the Almost Remembered', reprinted by permission of Bloodaxe Books Ltd from *Life By Drowning* by Jeni Couzyn (Bloodaxe Books, 1985) and 'The Damson', from *The Apple Fall* by Helen Dunmore (Bloodaxe Books, 1983); Joan Board for 'The Last Word' and 'A New Kind of Fruit'; Jonathan Cape Ltd for Margaret Atwood's 'Christmas Carols', from *True Stories* (1982); Carcanet Press Ltd for Edith Scovell's 'Song for a Young Mother' and 'Heavy As Lead', from *Collected Poems* (1988); Century Hutchinson Ltd for Irina Ratushinskaya's 'To the Children of Prison Warden Akimkina', from *Pencil Letters* (1989); Chatto & Windus for Carol Rumens' 'Moment of Faith', excerpted from 'A Birthday Sequence', from *From Berlin to Heaven* (1989); Margaret Crane for 'Rocks and Stones and Trees'; Curtis Brown Ltd (Australia) and Janet Frame for 'Yet Another Poem About a Dying Child' and Curtis Brown Ltd (New York) for Lucille Clifton's 'Lost Baby Poem', from *Good News About the Earth* (Random House, USA, 1972); Menna Elfyn for 'Reflection'; Gloria Escoffery for 'Twins', from *Loggerhead* (Sandberry Press, 1988, Jamaica); Faber & Faber for Anne Ridler's 'A Matter of Life and Death', from *New and Selected Poems* (1988); Pamela Gillilan for 'Threshold'; David Higham Associates Ltd for Elizabeth Jennings' 'The Unknown Child', 'Lazarus' and 'For a Child Born Dead', from *Collected Poems* (Macmillan, 1986) and Penelope Shuttle's 'The Conceiving' and 'The Silver Bridge' from *The Orchard Upstairs* (Oxford University Press, 1980); Olwyn Hughes for Sylvia Plath's 'Heavy Women', 'For a Fatherless Son' and extracts from 'Three Women', from *Collected Poems* (Faber, 1981), © Ted Hughes 1971, 1965 and 1981); Jezebel Tapes & Books for Marg Yeo's 'To Say Yes' from *Unnatural Acts* (1987); Biddy Jenkinson for 'Ciunas'; Karnak House for Grace Nichols' 'In My Name' from *I is a Long Memoried Woman* (1983); Lanny Kennish for 'On Birth' and 'Daughter Dark' from *The Brook Runs* (Wynstones Press); Dinah Livingstone for 'Woman of El Salvador' and 'Eschatological Dimension', from *Keeping Heart – Poems 1957–89* (Katabasis, 1989); 'Foetal Song' reprinted by permission of Louisiana State University Press from *Anonymous Sins* by Joyce Carol Oates. Copyright © 1969 by Lousiana State University Press; John Murray Ltd for Linda Pastan's 'Notes From a Delivery Room' and 'Journey's End', from *Selected Poems* (1979);

Methuen (London) for Michèle Roberts' 'Poem on a Midsummer's Day and 'Demeter Keeps Going' from *Mirror of the Mother* (1986); 'Who He Was' from *Collected Earlier Poems 1940–1960*. Copyright © 1959 by Denise Levertov. Reprinted by permission of New Direction Publishing Corporation. US and Canadian and UK and Commonwealth rights; 'Labour Pains' by Yosano Akiko. Kenneth Rexroth: *Women Poets of Japan*. Copyright © 1977 by Kenneth Rexroth and Ikuko Atsumi. Reprinted by permission of New Direction Publishing Corporation. US and Canadian and UK and Commonwealth rights; 'Broken Moon' by Carole Satyamurti, Copyright © Carole Satyamurti 1987. Reprinted from *Broken Moon* by Carole Satyamurti (1987) by permission of Oxford University Press; 'Tempo' by Lauris Edmond from *Selected Poems*, Copyright © Oxford University Press New Zealand, 1986; 'Death of a Young Son by Drowning' from *The Journals of Susanna Moodie* by Margaret Atwood. Copyright © Oxford University Press Canada 1970; Marion Pitman for 'I am the Barren Woman'; Polygon for Liz Lochhead's 'Everybody's Mother', from *Dreaming Frankenstein* (1984); Porcépic Books for Dorothy Livesay's 'Serenade for Strings', from *The Woman I Am* (1977); Joan Van Poznack for 'Motherfunk'; Raven Arts Press for Sara Berkeley's 'Seeding', *Penn*, (1986); Kathleen Raine for 'Spell of Creation' and 'Invocation II', from *Collected Poems* (Hamish Hamilton, 1956) and 'Change', from *The Presence* (Golgonooza, 1988); 'Poem to Ease Birth', from *A Book of Women Poets From Aniquity to Now*, edited by Aliki Barnstone and Willis Barnstone. Copyright © 1980 by Schocken Books, Inc. Reprinted by permission of Schocken Books, published by Pantheon Books, a Division of Random House, Inc.; Martin Secker & Warburg Ltd for Vicki Feaver's 'Children', from *Close Relatives* (1981) and Sandra Hochman's 'Elation after Childbirth' from *Earthworks* (1972); Seren Books for Christine Evans' 'Floating', from *Cometary Phases* (1989); 'For You, Who Didn't Know' by Nancy Willard Copyright © 1979 by Washington and Lee University, reprinted from *Shenandoah*: The Washington and Lee University Review, with the permission of the Editor; (Vol. 22, No. 3); Smithsonian Institute (Ethology) for 'Our Earth Mother', from *Zuni Ritual Poetry* by R. Bunzel; Stride and Taxus Press for Catherine Byron's 'She Promises Her Firstborn Daughters . . .' and 'The Black & Tans Deliver her Cousin's Son' (1985); 'O Wind of Tizoula' Reprinted by permission of the University of Texas Press from *Middle Eastern Muslim Women Speak*, edited by Elizabeth W. Fernea and Basima Q. Bezirgan, 1977; Ruth Valentine for 'Infertility'; Virago Press for Grace Nichols' 'Praise Song for My Mother' from *Fat Black Women's Poems* Copyright © Grace Nichols. Published by Virago Press 1984 and Astra's Fantasy Mother' from *Back You Come, Mother Dear* Copyright © Astra. Published by Virago Press 1986; 'Danae' Copyright © 1959 by Barbara Howes, reprinted from *Light and Dark*, by permission of Wesleyan University Press; Ira Wolfert for Helen Wolfert's 'Woman Against the Moon'; The Women's Press for Anna Swir's 'The Midwife' and 'Her Belly' from *Fat Like the Sun* (1986) translated by Margaret Marshment; and Evan Zimroth for 'Planting Children, 1939' and 'Breathing'.

'Child of Our Time' by Eavan Boland appeared in *The War Horse* (Arlen House, 1980); Irina Ratushinskaya's 'To the Children of Prison Warden Akimkina' appeared in *Pencil Letters* (Bloodaxe, 1986); 'The Unborn' by Gerda Mayer appeared in *AND 3 & Monkey on the Analyst's Couch* (Ceolfrith Press, 1980): 'The Sea at Dawn' by Pascale Petit appeared in *Angels of Fire*, ed. Sylvia Paskin and Jay Ramsay (Chatto & Windus, *1985*) and also in *Strange Mathematics* and *New Poetry 11 Pen*; 'The Birth of Vahakri' appeared in *Anthology of Armenian Verse*, ed. D. Der Hovanessian and M. Margossian, (Columbia University Press, 1978); 'To the Newborn' by Judit Tóth appeared in *Modern Hungarian Verse*, ed. Miklós Vajda (Columbia University Press, 1977); 'Persephone' by Karen Whiteson appeared in *Feminist Review*, Winter 1984; 'Separations' by Jean Janzen appeared in *Three Mennonite Poets* (Good Books, 1986); 'Lost' and 'Woman in a Tableau' by Katherine Gallagher appeared in *Passengers to the City* (Hale and Ironmonger, 1985), the former also in *The Age* and the latter in *Writing Women*; 'The Abortion' and 'Unknown Girl in a Maternity Ward' by Anne Sexton appeared in *All My Pretty Ones* (1962), and 'Pain for a Daughter' in *Live or Die* (Houghton Mifflin (1966); 'Rosie' by Moira Andrew appeared in *Light the Blue Touch Paper* (Iron Press, 1986); 'Woman of El Salvador' and 'Eschatological Dimension' by Dinah Livingstone appeared in *Keeping Heart – Poems 1967–89* (Katabasis, 1989) and 'Oxytocin' by Susan Taylor appeared in *The Complete Bearded Stranger* (Lincs and Humberside Arts); 'Early Developments' and 'Three Months Have Gone' by Pat Borthwick appeared in *Between Clouds and Caves* (Littlewood Press, 1988); 'Praise of a Child' in *The Moon Cannot Fight*, ed. U. Beier and B. Gbadmosi (Mbari Publications); *'The Calling Up', 'Dream Drumming'* and *'To Enter that Rhythm Where the Soul is Lost'* by Muriel Rukeyser appeared in *Collected Poems* (McGraw Hill, 1982); 'Motherfunk' by Joan van Poznack appeared in *Open Poetry Conventicle* 1; 'I am the Barren Woman' by Marion Pitman appeared in *Other Poetry* 24, and 'Lunch with Veronica' (Eating People, 1988); 'Planting Children–1939' by Evan Zimroth appeared in *Early Ripening*, ed. Marge Piercy (Pandora, 1989); 'This Belonging, This Us' by Elaine Randell appeared in *Beyond All Other* (Pig Press); 'A Cycle of Women' by Sharon Barba and 'Woman Against the Moon' by Helen Wolfert appeared in *Rising Tides*, ed. Laura Chester and Sharon Barba (Pocket Books, 1973); 'The New Door' by Pippa Little and 'Tapping the Deep' by Pascale Petit appeared in *Poetry Review*; 'Reflection' by Menna Elfyn appeared in *Poetry Wales* 22.3 under the title 'I Love my Children More than Anyone'; 'Fallow' by Susan Taylor appeared in *Prospice*; 'Natural High' by Jean Binta Breeze appeared in *Riddym Ravings* (Race Today Publications, 1988); 'Pilgrim Woman' by Pippa Little appeared in *Transformation*, ed. Jay Ramsay (Rivelin Grapheme, 1988); 'Abortion' by Valerie Sinason appeared in *Smoke*; 'Birth Stories' by Ger Duffy and 'Scream' by Susan Taylor appeared in *Spare Rib*, Aug 89; 'Rocks and Stones and Trees' by

Acknowledgments

Margaret Crane appeared in *Stand*, Spring 85, under the title 'After-Effects'; 'The Last Word' and 'A New Kind of Fruit' by Joan Board appeared in *Stride* 22; 'Knowing' by Mary Coghill, and 'Rebirth' by Catriona Stamp appeared in *Bread and Roses* ed. Diana Scott (Virago, 1982); 'The Voice of the Woman' by Pat V. T. West is the final section from *The Crumbles (The Wasteland Rewritten);* 'For Marion' by Judith Bollinger appeared in *Waterchild* (Wildwood House, 1981); 'Birth 16 ix 78' and 'Mother's Catalogue' by Lesley Saunders appeared in *Why Children?* The Women's Press, 1980); 'Seeding' by Sara Berkeley and 'Ciunas' by Biddy Jenkinson appeared in *Pillars of the House*, ed. A. A. Kelly (Wolfhound, 1987); and 'To My Sister' by Jenny Vuglar appeared in *Writing Women* Vol. 7, 1.

Every effort has been made to trace the original copyright holders, but in some instances this has not been possible. It is hoped that any such omission from this list will be excused.

INTRODUCTION

There are many anthologies today, on varied subjects – some of universal interest, others marginal – but almost nothing on the subject of birth. It is surely a miracle, a rite of passage as significant as love and death, yet when I came to this experience in my own life and avidly sought poems on this theme I found them few and far between and certainly not readily available. I slowly came to collect a number of fine poems and shared them with others until I had enough substance for an anthology. This coincided with the discovery and development of my own creativity, a process very much like birth, with a painful labour, explosion of writing and fear of flying the nest.

Contemporary poetry has more often than not become cerebral, self-referential and word-centred. This anthology tries to root poetry in the great physical and inner transformations of birth and its aftermath; it seeks to celebrate but doesn't shirk the cost of bearing, nurturing and suffering child loss.

Talking about birth in our society has largely been seen as distasteful, and motherhood as mundane; something private not public, belonging to women's sphere, unclean even. I have been given the distinct impression in literary circles that writing about it is a stage you go through before returning to 'more important things'. This is to miss an obvious truth – that birth is, and represents, the principle of life, that all things have a source, a moment of creation and taking on of being; that birth resonates throughout life in many different forms – it is a metaphor for all changes that generate new states. This includes physical change, awakening of creativity, self-discovery, political revolution and spiritual rebirth.

I have tried to include poems reflecting a variety of experience, styles and levels of meaning. The women poets represented here are mostly English and contemporary, with a fair selection of American and Commonwealth poets, and there are also a number of foreign language poets as well as poems from traditional sources. Above all I wanted good quality, originality and breadth of perspective. The anthology is arranged in seven sections, which reflect birth as an organic process having distinct stages: *Conceiving* – the seed, the idea, that is sown; *Forming* – a slow hidden growth and taking shape of child and vision; *Labour* – pain

and struggle; *Birth* – a breakthrough and breaking out; *Newborn* –
a new creation, death of the old, birth of the new, a separate
being with a life of its own; *Motherhood* – the complex task of
the nurturer, fraught with ambiguity and conflict as well as great
joy; and, perhaps hardest of all, *Letting Go* – with its attendant
separation, loss and change.

I received a huge response to the project and felt very privileged
to receive such excellent and heartfelt work. Many letters
expressed interest and the need for such a book. Some women
specifically set about recalling and writing their experiences and
some found that writing changed a negative experience into a
positive one. Compiling this book was like dipping into a rich
and varied brew, and it was hard to make final choices and to
bring them into a balanced and meaningful sequence. I hope this
has been achieved. In stark, spare language or with vivid and
intense imagery, these poems depict an entrance into an amazing,
sometimes frightening world with no known landmarks, a jour-
ney where there is no going back. So too, the interior journey –
the breaking of the old and the emerging of the new.

Finally, I hope that more work will come out of this, whether
anthologies, prose or single collections. I have no doubt that the
value, the interest and the audience are there. The title, taken
from Penelope Shuttle's poem 'The Conceiving' refers here to
both mother and child, as they are symbiotically united; the
experience is in the flesh, yet also carries the quality of gold –
precious and enduring.

ROSEMARY PALMEIRA

CONCEIVING

Stir Of Ripeness

Spell of Creation

Within the flower there lies a seed,
Within the seed there springs a tree,
Within the tree there spreads a wood.

In the wood there burns a fire,
And in the fire there melts a stone,
Within the stone a ring of iron.

Within the ring there lies an O
Within the O there looks an eye,
In the eye there swims a sea,

And in the sea reflected sky,
And in the sky there shines the sun,
Within the sun a bird of gold.

Within the bird there beats a heart,
And from the heart there flows a song,
And in the song there sings a word.

In the word there speaks a world,
A word of joy, a world of grief,
From joy and grief there springs my love.

Oh love, my love, there springs a world,
And on the world there shines a sun
And in the sun there burns a fire,

Within the fire consumes my heart
And in my heart there beats a bird,
And in the bird there wakes an eye,

Within the eye, earth, sea and sky,
Earth, sky and sea within an O
Lie like the seed within the flower.

KATHLEEN RAINE

Our Earth Mother

That our earth mother may wrap herself
In a fourfold robe of white meal;
That she may be covered with frost flowers;
That yonder on all the mossy mountains,
The forests may huddle together with the cold;
That their arms may be broken by the snow,
In order that the land may be thus,
I have made my prayer sticks into living beings.

When our earth mother is replete with living waters,
When spring comes,
The source of our flesh,
All the different kinds of corn,
We shall lay to rest in the ground.
With their earth mother's living waters,
They will be made into new beings.
Coming out standing into the daylight
Of their sun father,
Calling for rain,
To all sides they will stretch out their hands.
Then from wherever the rain-makers stay quietly
They will send forth their misty breath;
Their massed clouds filled with water will come out to sit down
    with us;
Far from their homes,
With outstretched hands of water they will embrace the corn,
Stepping down to caress them with their fresh waters,
With their fine rain caressing the earth,
With their heavy rain caressing the earth,
And yonder, wherever the roads of the rain-makers come forth,
Torrents will rush forth,
Silt will rush forth,
Mountains will be washed out,
Logs will be washed down,
Yonder all the mossy mountains
Will drip with water.
The clay-lined hollows of our earth mother
Will overflow with water,

From all the lakes
Will rise the cries of the children of the rain-makers,
In all the lakes
There will be joyous dancing –
Desiring that it should be thus,
I send forth my prayers.

That our earth mother
May wear a fourfold green robe,
Full of moss,
Full of flowers,
Full of pollen,
That the land may be thus
I have made you into living beings.

ANON *(Zuni Prayer, Pueblo Indian, N. America)*

Song: The Calling-Up

Rumour, stir of ripeness
rising within this girl
sensual, blossoming
of meaning, its light and form.

The birth-cry summoning
out of the male, the father
from the warm woman
a mother in response.

The word of death
calls up the fight with stone
wrestle with grief with time
from the material make
an art harder than bronze.

MURIEL RUKEYSER

Apple

Eve picked the first apple,
We, the most recent, in complicity.
Was it an apple, ripened with rain and sun
Or a pithy pomegranate, calling for a good delve
Or an apricot, swollen gold and honey velvet?

Repeated deaths of this flesh
Snatched our breath from one another.
Sunlight entered spaces in between our intimacy
A misensemble of heads of limbs.

We understood.

GEORGINA LOCK

Woman to Man

The eyeless labourer in the night,
the selfless, shapeless seed I hold,
builds for its resurrection day –
silent and swift and deep from sight
foresees the unimagined light.

This is no child with a child's face;
this has no name to name it by:
yet you and I have known it well.
This is our hunter and our chase,
the third who lay in our embrace.

This is the strength that your arm knows,
the arc of flesh that is my breast,
the precise crystals of our eyes.
This is the blood's wild tree that grows
the intricate and folded rose.

This is the maker and the made;
this is the question and reply;
the blind head butting at the dark,
the blaze of light along the blade.
Oh hold me, for I am afraid.

JUDITH WRIGHT

The Unknown Child

That child will never lie in me, and you
Will never be its father. Mirrors must
Replace the real image, make it true
So that the gentle love-making we do
Has powerful passions and a parent's trust.

The child will never lie in me and make
Our loving careful. We must kiss and touch
Quietly, watch our own reflexions break
As in a pool that is disturbed. Oh take
My watchful love; there must not be too much.

A child lies within my mind. I see
the eyes, the hands. I see you also there.
I see you waiting with an honest care,
Within my mind, within me bodily,
And birth and death close to us constantly.

ELIZABETH JENNINGS

Who He Was

One is already here whose life
bearing like seed its distant death, shall grow
through human pain, human joy, shall know
music and weeping, only because

the strange flower of your thighs
bloomed in my body. From our joy
begins a stranger's history. Who
is this rider in the dark? We lie
in candlelight; the child's quick unseen movements
jerk my belly under your hand. Who
conceived in joy, in joy,
lies nine months alone in a walled silence?

Who is this rider in the dark,
nine months the body's tyrant,
nine months alone in a walled silence
our minds cannot fathom?
Who is it will come out of the dark,
whose cries demand our mercy, tyrant
no longer, but alone still, in a solitude
memory cannot reach?
Whose lips will suckle at these breasts,
thirsting, unafraid for life?
Whose eyes will look out of that solitude?

The wise face of the unborn
ancient and innocent
must change to infant ignorance
before we see it, irrevocable third
looking into our lives; the child
must hunger, sleep, cry, gaze, long weeks
before it learns of laughter. Love can never
wish a life no darkness; but may love
be constant in the life our love has made.

DENISE LEVERTOV

Seeding

The shuttle works onwards from winter's backward draw
Springtide washing driftwood high on her sighblown beach
The woman waits, tight-limbed,
Time-dried, for her babies to begin.

Other circles weave revolving arcs into her day
Splitting a pea-pod – the tiny explosion
Of ripe, tense seeds, spiralling back along the wind-curved edge
The floating time seeds of the dandelion
And burdocks fuzz the grass, sycamore on a dizzy wing,
False fruits of her pangless labour.

A myriad of scattered grains
When the stamen bends with belly full
And swelling buds listen
To the easy breath of blood-veined leaf
In the rhythmic black-blue, black-blue night
And tenuous quivering light.

Wider circles weave their shadows on the earth
High on the brow, wind-dried, hardly bruised
With handling – the fruit of no rain.

Early morning draws water from the driest eyes
In crop and field, waiting woman drinks from thin air
Tasting dry in her mouth, the seed quiet
Deep in her virgin earth where winter leaves
The trees bare.

SARA BERKELEY

I am the Barren Woman

I am the barren woman
the discarded
the sour field
the blunt knife no whetstone can hone
the fruit fallen unripe
the cracked pot
when times come to an edge
I shall first feel its sharpness
a lean year spares no meat
for the belly that will not quicken.

MARION PITMAN

from Three Women

THIRD VOICE:

I remember the minute when I knew for sure.
The willows were chilling,
The face in the pool was beautiful, but not mine –
It had a consequential look, like everything else,
And all I could see was dangers: doves and words,
Stars and showers of gold – conceptions, conceptions!
I remember a white, cold wing

And the great swan, with its terrible look,
Coming at me, like a castle, from the top of the river.
There is a snake in swans.
He glided by; his eye had a black meaning.
I saw the world in it – small, mean and black,
Every little word hooked to every little word, and act to act.
A hot blue day had budded into something.

I wasn't ready. The white clouds rearing
Aside were dragging me in four directions.
I wasn't ready.
I had no reverence.
I thought I could deny the consequence –
But it was too late for that. It was too late, and the face
Went on shaping itself with love, as if I was ready.

SYLVIA PLATH

This

this stone weight in the pit of the gut
this rough filling of an empty space
this smouldering vat of love
this cavern, this cave
this drowning wave
this sucking sponge
this crawling hunger
this pursing thirst

this overwhelming, undermining urge
this surge of hope
this dream of unreserved devotion
this insatiable emotion
this crying need
this dying feeling
this desire for a child . . .

KATIE CAMPBELL

O Wind of Tizoula

O wind of Tizoula, O wind of Amsoud!
Blow over the plains and over the sea,
Carry, oh carry my thoughts
To him who is so far, so far,
And who has left me without a little child.
O wind! Remind him I have no child.

O wind of Tizoula, O wind of Amsoud!
Blow away that desire for riches
That sends our young men away
And makes them forget the girls they've married, their mothers,
And the old ones left in the village.
O wind! Remind him I have no child.

ANON (Berber Woman's Song)

from To the Children of Prison Warden Akimkina

It had snowed for four whole days.
The girls froze in their cell.
They weren't very old; the eldest
Was twenty-one, no more.
'Madam,' they said 'At least
Pour us some boilding water!
And couldn't you give us some tights
If we've got to sit on the floor?'

'You bitches,' came the reply:
'So what else would you like?
You'd get nothing, if I had my way,
You scroungers, not one bite.
D'you want some bedclothes, some boots?
If I had my way, you pigs,
You'd be in your birthday suits.'
Of course, they deserved this lot.
They were lucky not to get worse.
The bosses don't make mistakes
And put you inside without cause.
It's winter, so let them freeze.
Why should their stoves be hot?
That's what SHIZO's[1] all about:
They won't be back in a hurry.
It's not as if they're naked:
They've got their prison-smocks.
And they haven't much time to do
Anyway, so why worry?
They're already worn out. They lie
On the floor, in spite of the cold,
While the prison mice fearlessly
Scamper across their faces.
Nobody's died. They'll be freed
After a spell in SHIZO.
Don't waste your sympathy.
They're invalids, not war-heroes.
Some will get out in ten days,
Some in a fortnight or less.
And if a short spell below zero's
Injured their health, who cares?
It's part of the punishment.
Let them serve their time, and then
They can go somewhere for treatment.
We've got problems of our own.
The fact that they can't have children
Is something they still don't know.
If you think clearly about it,

1. Punishment cell.

It's none of their business to know.
Of course, it will all come out later.
They'll go from doctor to doctor,
Frantic with hope, as they try
To work out their dates, but mistaken.
They'll cry in the corridors
Of countless maternity clinics.
Through endless appointments they'll cry,
And at night a thin voice will wake them:
'Are you listening, Mummy?
Listen, listen to me.
Do you remember you dreamt
That you'd given birth to me?
Now the mice, the grey mice
Have eaten me up.
Where are you,
Where are you,
Where were you then?
Mummy, mummy, I'm cold.
Put me a nappy on.
I'm frightened of being alone.
Why don't you come to me?
You wanted a baby girl
Remember?
Remember?
Why don't you come
Why don't you?
Aren't you even waiting for me?'
But what, in fact, really happened?
Plenty of others are crying
In the maternity home
We have no shortage of people.
There are millions and millions of them.
We can find people to build
Factories, furnaces, shops;
People who'll do what they're told
And people who'll get to the top.
It isn't so bad, after all . . .

IRINA RATUSHINSKAYA

Dancing

In the middle of the class
on the floor, dancing
suddenly I remember the child.

O where is my child?

A voice breaks through the air
which only I hear
but everyone stops dancing.

Am I not barren?

Music urges me on.
My feet, head, heart bear
the stone which keeps beating.

My child is not here.
My child is not dancing.
Dancing I carry the barren.

JOAN MICHELSON

The Unborn

The queen in her garden
walked through the high grass
and found an infant prince
in an egg of blue grass.

Not the sun's down feathers
in that deep green nest,
nor the warmth of the queen's arms,
nor the heat of her breast,

could awaken that child
which sleeping lay
in his blue ice-coffin
at bright mid-day.

GERDA MAYER

Tricked

The idea, worn smooth with thought, accepted
Swerving currents towards a future.
Yet now the body tricks me
With its whispers of easy fertility
Glimpsed in others:
Those who, they say,
First time, they say,
And women whose lives drip with babies.
I suspect a resistance
In the silence processes and
Their deception of youth;
A rhythm too long unhindered,
Too late to trip the cycle.
Try to learn its secrets,
To stem the ebbing chances
But in some dark, unknown place
Time ripens for the bursting egg
To split free and rush headlong
Clenched against life.

SALLY MEYER

Bound in Blue

at thirty i had her bound in
blue, with gold lettering down the spine.

the examiners, both male,
complimented me on her presentation and
weighed her in as a ph. d.

a bookcase served as a crib
while i chased tenure and the perks that go with it,
a crèche on campus and maternity leave.

three years and three temporary contracts later
a doctor explains
that the fibrous lump in the patient's womb will,
of course, make conception extremely difficult.

smiling to myself i fumble for
the letter offering publication;
tonight i start knitting.

PENNY SUMNER

To My Unborn Daughter

forbid you
I never could . . .

you simply didn't
happen

and so you are

hungers
I never stilled

countries
I never saw

moon
that never lit my room
from within the pane

the crossed sum
I can not put right

one self
I'll never recognise

safe
anchored

inside your
singularity

if you passed me on the
spume

I didn't even notice

MAGGIE MOUNTFORD

Danaë

Golden, within this golden hive
Wild bees drone,
As if at any moment they may
Swarm and be gone
From the arched fibres of their cage,
Lithe as whalebone.

Over a pasture, once, I saw
A flock of small
Martins flying in concert, high
Then wheeling, fall;
Like buckshot pent in a string bag
They dotted all

That sky-patch, holding form in their flight,
A vase poured,
Their breathing shape hung in the air –
Below, the road
Fled secretly as quicksilver:
My eyes blurred.

All things come to their pinnacle
Though landscapes shift,
Women sit in the balance, as
Upon a knife;
Irony cuts to the quick – is this
Life or new life?

They sit their years out on a scale,
The heavy yoke
Of their heavy stomachs grounding them –
Or else come back
To barrenness with each full moon;
Minds go slack

Longing, or dreading, that a new
Form will take shape.
(The martins' swarming is a brush-stroke
On the landscape,
Within their white-gold, fleshly hall
The wild bees wake.)

Homing at close of day, they meet
This moment: now:
Love calls from its subterranean passage,
The bed they know
May support agony or joy –
To bed they go.

BARBARA HOWES

The Heir

How we prepared for you. Nights
carefully, we would climb
into the long darkness
where you were lurking
made for you new
arms and head and
small new body to begin again in.
Nights out of our love for each other
we made you that small body.
We created it, meticulous, patiently.
How we were God making it.
It was perfect. A house. A safe
house to be at ease in.

Clasped on the verge
of the desert where you walk
how we called out your name
that we were ready.
We called out your name
where you were withered and poison
in the shedded dark.

From the edge, the brink
You watch us without eyes.
The softness of bodies the warm
house we have prepared for you.
You would leap across the darkness
but you have no body.
You would weep
but you have no voice.
You would cry out to us to
come
and find you, but we can't hear.

You watch us call you without eyes.
O here there is no way in.
Here is all flesh and hard bone.
Child.
They are pouring bandages on your
broken house.

JENI COUZYN

Woman

I have come upon a spell of stillness
out of the mainstream current
a little bay, a sheltered pocket
visited by boat and sea.
The water surges up, searching its mark
carving its furrows, ebbing away.
The bay stretches and resounds
in scalloped rings upon the sands.
Lost to sight now the lone stroke
of the swimmer on the high seas;
the cove curls around its own curve
pondering, brooding, waiting.

★   ★   ★

I am already making a space
my belly a rich loamy lining
a warm hollow, a barrel of grain
a grass-thick valley, a nestful of birds
a bowl of still water, a whirling eddy
a vat full of wine, a chalice of grail
an eye full of tear, a bay full of sea
a well earth-deep, a bell of bronze.

The whole of my cupped life
is streaming slowly through me
down the glass-green shaft;
all possibilities and impossibilities
array themselves before me –
I prepare myself to bear a mystery.

ROSEMARY PALMEIRA

The Conceiving
(for Zoe)

Now
You are in the ark of my blood
in the river of my bones
in the woodland of my muscles
in the ligaments of my hair
in the wit of my hands
in the smear of my shadow
in the armada of my brain
under the stars of my skull
in the arms of my womb
Now you are here
you worker in the gold of flesh

PENELOPE SHUTTLE

FORMING
Curiously Wrought

The Full Moon Rises

The full moon rises
Yet my head is clean
I go to the well
The full moon rises
The fish rejoice in the deep pool of Koeli-Kachhar
Branches of the mango grove bend low to the earth.

Moon of the second month casts its shadow
There is a new bud in the garden
My lord desires me for the scent of my flower.

Moon of the third month casts its shadow
The life within me desires strange food
I long for mud and kodon dirt.

Moon of the fourth month casts its shadow
With gifts my mother comes for Sidauri
I sit in her lap and eat the seven foods.

Moon of the fifth months casts its shadow
The secret life stirs within me
O my darling I can hear your heartbeats.

Moon of the sixth month casts its shadow
When they catch it, we will know if it is saur or kotri
Moon of the sixth month casts its shadow.

Moon of the seventh month casts its shadow
Black are my nipples – it will be my father
My belly is long – it will be my mother.

Moon of the eighth month casts its shadow
The hour approaches, my husband comes no more near me
I saw a snake in my path and it went away blinded.

Moon of the ninth month casts its shadow
How weary is the life within; when it sees its dark prison
It struggles to be free and make its camp on earth.

ANON (*Indian Folk Song translated by V. Elwin*)

from **Woman Against the Moon**

The preparation of the body

I stand mute in the moonshine and lights of the moon
That go over my body are fingers that change
Once again what I am, a warm statue of a woman
That stood steadfast already, supreme and complete.

I stood slim and myself in the moon, but the fingers
Have added warm clay to my limbs and have made
Them like brown earthen jars and as if they were flooded
with milk and honey and gold oil of palm.
My two breasts that were fine and as white as are mushrooms
Are now covered with honey, and fingers of moon
Have rounded them as with the pulp of a fruit.
  This is honey, milk and yellow broom of rye,
  It is bush and pomegranate, but not I.
  It is Venus and her blossom flesh upon
  my immaculately sculpted skeleton.
  It is Mother Ceres plowing wider lanes
  Through my needle-narrow and pin-pointed veins.
  It is apples cumulus upon the tree,
  It is earth and grass the moon has made of me.

HELEN WOLFERT

Pregnant Woman Speaks to the Sea

        She says:
        come, sea
        make a cave of me

        hollow me
        like this slim blue shell

        empty me
        like this broken egg
        dropped cold and round
        on these rocks

return me
to myself
like the tides

come, sea
make a shell of me
free me
wash me

JILL DAWSON

Full Sail

Remember the sailing barges,
with their swelled,
blood–coloured canvas?
How they bore down–river,
sails whipping and flapping,
as the wind controlled
their matrons' progress.
In those pre–war days,
the merest hint of fullness
was a gross affront.
I walked in the wake
of these proud vessels,
carrying their cargo
to a pre–ordained destination,
from which there was
no turning back.

ROSE BURNETT

Heavy Women

Irrefutable, beautifully smug
As Venus, pedestalled on a half-shell
Shawled in blonde hair and salt
Scrim of a sea breeze, the women
Settle in their belling dresses.
Over each weighty stomach a face
Floats calm as a moon or a cloud.

Smiling to themselves, they meditate
Devoutly as the Dutch bulb
Forming its twenty petals
The dark still nurses its secret.
On the green hill, under the thorn trees,
They listen for the millennium,
the knock of the small, new heart.

SYLVIA PLATH

The Eschatological Dimension

Pregnant woman cannot reach her feet.
She is a barrel.
Her fellow carefully rolls her about.
He's in bed with a whale.
He likes her like that.

On a good day she can understand
the astonishing thought
that Origen taught
that glorified bodies are perfectly round.

DINAH LIVINGSTONE

Expectant

Child come of a snowflake,
you danced first in the cloud of a turning year
when only slightly bigger than a footprint.
Now lambs are thundering in wide spaces,
you gallop and play inside,
with sharp movements, test how far you can shake me.
My life reshapes in your tiny unfinished hands.
I warm to the task in the rapid grass.
I knit the sun into small white sleeves.

Day by day, you brand your namelessness
upon my heart.
Night by night, my blood leaps
with your weight tied in me.
You curl your hands round my flanks
and bounce your neat hips upwards;
rider in my belly,
cowboy of seahorses,
mermaid.
Lover of unknown gender,
do not rush to come into my arms
I swell to the size of your life.
Keep me this way
as long as you want.

SUSAN TAYLOR

Not Beautiful

I cry
and turn away
from films
which months ago
had made me sneer,
my mind mimics
an awkward body

clumsy with the changes.
Emotions, gawky as schoolgirls,
make me absurd, not beautiful.
You ask what's wrong
I cannot say
do not know
except the strength of sadness
scares me.

LOUISE HUDSON

Resting

It is now part of my night
      waking up to darkness.
It floods out now
      this sea of black water. Soon
at the birth
my night time shall be all awakeness
      and the blackness of night
shall be the coming of the baby, pushed
and pushed
      and pushed
till it is out.

Like a ripe plum
my soft skin is swelling and thinning. Soon
new flesh will push out.
      And now it is gradual
a gentle walk through the flood meadows.
      When I am tired
I lie down and rest
and darkness in day is part of me.

      Still beyond
out the flower dotted grasses, Silbury rises.
The steep climb to the top will be
      an acute ascent.

Muscles will hot up with breathlessness
the compacted earth will split open
the birth of this moment
      the sky presenting with a thudding darkness, now
are only intimations.

SARA BOYES

Seek Not to Hold Her

Seek not to hold her
for she is given
to the bees.

Her breasts are two
white roses
dispensing sweet nectar

and the ripening fruit
of her womb is what the world
waits for –
in the patient eyes
of her lover
and in the flaming palms
of supplicants
starving, under the Indian
sun.

Seek not to hold her
for she will give birth
among the bees, alone
in the wilderness

and when she passes
wide winged
with her precious progeny –
on the windswept soil
which has forgotten

how to weep
you will hear the
fresh dew falling.

JEHANNE MEHTA

Knowing

I dug in with all the spirit of spring
delightfully teased by the sweet scent
of the fresh turned soil – earth meets sun
for the first time – darkness to warmth and light.
Let lie and sleep for the frost to work
and snow and rain and in due time
plough, fold in, nurturance of secrecy:
I have the seeds, given over and over
stored and harboured, grains of now and ever
planted and I catch my breath, I let
the west wind welcome first and breathe
only after as memory of beckoner.

You grew, I grew, bathed in sun, balmed
by warmth, hallowed round in rain and my
thoughts echo and cradle the harmony:
all this I cannot change and watch,
in the heat and the waiting, turn,
we all turn and see that the moon harbours
all that we ever need to know:
we all have a harvest to reap –
I have sharpened and refined
caressed the waiting over, and now
I cut all growth and stem and yield
the fruit, or head, or heart, or ears
and I listen: oh sister – where is
the granary? I am a winnow sieve and
without you all the grains will fall through.

MARY COGHILL

Nearly

Wind grasps its first leaves in a fist
tugs them from twigs,
lets them find their own way down.
Limp yellow, not yet crisp, they follow
incline of hillside, settle in ditch.
Grasps, too, the acorn
spiralling its load in an arc,
dropping it – flac! – on the matt earth.

Round as a belly this oak fruit,
smooth, and tucked in its cup;
the weight of it gleams green against damp.
Stripped from branch, its two halves
are a whole, holding close,
each bound to other still,
still inseparable.

ZANNA BESWICK

Early Developments

I am the acrobatic fish in your dark bowl.
In tightening water I gulp your red fern.
Cramped as a tadpole in spawn
I flick my tail against your taut drum
to the soft lilt of fiddles
and tin-whistle tunes.

My fins have shrunk back.
The plates of my skull lie open.
Sounds drift into shapes.

From under your fine linen apron
a cat is its purr
a spoon is its tinkling
books are the tick of a clock
and tones in your throat.

When an engine cuts
or footsteps knock
your songs halt mid–note
then I see drowned sailors
swirled by the tide
tapping at portholes
tangled in nets.

Already I learn to tread water.

PAT BORTHWICK

Foetal Song

The vehicle gives a lurch but seems
to know its destination.
In here, antique darkness. I guess at things.
Tremors of muscles communicate
secrets to me. I am nourished.
A surge of blood pounding sweet
blossoms my gentle head.
I am perfumed wax melted of holy candles
I am ready to be fingered and shaped.

This cave unfolds to my nudge, which
seems gentle but is hard as steel.
Coils of infinite steel are my secret.
Within this shadowless cave I am not confused
I think I am a fish, or a small seal.
I have an impulse to swim, but without
moving; *she* moves and I drift after. . . .
I am a trout silent and gilled, a tiny seal
a slippery monster knowing all secrets.
Where is she off to now? – in high heels.
I don't like the jiggle of high heels.
On the street we hear horns, drills, feel sleeves,
feel rushes of language moving by
and every stranger has possibly
my father's face.

Now we are in bed.
Her heart breathes quiet and I drink blood.
I am juicy and sweet and coiled.
Her dreams creep upon me through nightmare slots of windows
I cringe from them, unready.
I don't like such pictures.
Morning . . . and the safety of the day brings us
bedroom slippers, good.
Day at home, comfort in this sac,
three months from my birthday I dream
upon songs and eerie music, angels' flutes
that tear so stern upon earthly anger
(now they are arguing again).
Jokes and unjokes, married couple,
they clutch each other in water
I feel him nudge me but it is by accident.
The darkness of their sacs must be slimy with dead tides
and hide what they knew of ponds and knotty ropes of lilies.

It forsakes them now, cast into the same bed.
The tide throws them relentlessly into the same bed.
While he speaks to her I suck marrow from her bones.
It has a grainy white taste, a little salty.
Oxygen from her tremendous lungs tastes white too
but airy bubbly, it makes me dizzy . . . !

She speaks to him and her words do not matter.
Marrow and oxygen matter eternally. They are mine.
Sometimes she walks on concrete, my vehicle,
sometimes on gravel, on grass, on the
blank worn tides of our floors at home.
She and he, months ago, decided not to kill me.
I rise and fall now like seaweed fleshed to fish, a surprise.
I am grateful.
I am waiting for my turn.

JOYCE CAROL OATES

Tapping the Deep

I dial infinity
tap lines through space,
might begin a story of the Tempest
in a sea of sleep, where the Id keens –
giant squid dreaming of souls in ships;
or Grandmother hooks on to the line
her words shrimp-faint,
the cord sundances

the gap between our years.
I dial further and find
Mother knitting me skins
to be born in
I can hear the click-click
echoing down time,
her unravelling them
at the end of each skein,

then her fall from Earth
and quest for sanity –
the lifebuoy sighted but never reached –
matrix for the fathom of her mind,
Isle of the Blessed
where even the mad rest
and Caliban is caged –
my singing sends her there.

The telephone is a searchlight
on this clear night,
even God mumbles in an excuse
for the state of things,
and the doctor's verdict is negative
so that the dead are reprieved.
There is no static of machine-gun fire
no radiant cloud, no storm

but I know I can only be born
to mother again through wreckage,
exiled as she is. I am Ariel.
I transmit messages,
and I talk only when happy,
you can hear my music
when the wires cross
otherwise I don't exist.

PASCALE PETIT

Woman to Child

You who were darkness warmed my flesh
where out of darkness rose the seed.
Then all a world I made in me;
all the world you hear and see
hung upon my dreaming blood.

There moved the multitudinous stars
and coloured birds and fishes moved.
There swam the sliding continents.
All time lay rolled in me, and sense,
and love knew not its beloved.

O node and focus of the world;
I hold you deep within that well
you shall escape and not escape –
that mirrors still your sleeping shape;
that nurtures still your crescent cell.

I wither and you break from me;
yet though you dance in living light
I am the earth, I am the root,
I am the stem that fed the fruit,
the link that joins you to the night.

JUDITH WRIGHT

The Alfred Jewel[1]

With
huge black eyes
one curl of nostril and blur
mouth, your cry of beseeching
has caught up my heart. Green robed
tiny sea-god, you swim in lapis lazuli
your white bud hands clutch flowering rods
imprisoned foetus, you flail inside the
crystal rock, in the encrustation of gold.
How you sparkle in your teardrop womb!
You move me strangely. As if some
familiar child were calling,
calling to me from within.
And are you that Saxon
king, or his exiled
Christ, or my own
unborn, twelve
hundred years
old, who is
trying to
speak?

ROSEMARY PALMEIRA

Abortion

I

The girl in the
hot bath

white
as an egg

1. Anglo-Saxon pendant

is waiting for
the speck inside her

to boil

to death

II

In a few years
the girl will become
a wife
a sure-hearted mother
of planned children

She will gently lower her elbow
into a duckfilled bath
to check its temperature

III

But how does one explain later,
that is what I am asking,

How does one say to a might-have-been

'You came when we called
when the rich seas swam in our eyes
you came in the fish leaping season
when we were too young

and we met you with nets and murder
your speck of a fish-face
floundering in the red river

we were not ready for you then
and when we were ready
it was not you.
We are sorry.

You are not the first that had to die
coming in the wrong season, the wrong time.'

IV

The woman lying in the white bath
brown and speckled as an egg
rocks and floats on a small murder

There is a price she has paid
for her clear-eyed children.

VALERIE SINASON

Three Months Have Gone
(for Vega)

Starched white aprons
wrapped around my bed.
A most unusual mistiming,
an oversight,
they said you were not born
my little one, my almost born,
my little nameless fish.
But since,
your face peeps out all over this house,
outside this house,
cemented into the brickwork,
crayoned across the clouds.

When I stand at the nursery window
you are there,
cradled in the branches of the apple trees,
the moon leaning across
to thread you with white ribbons.

In the kitchen garden
I hear you whimpering
among the closed hearts of the lettuces,
your fisting hands reach out,
pull my fingers down to suck on.
I am rooted in this lettuce patch
for half a day or more
or for however long it takes.

Stained glass streams into the hall
cathedraling your pram.
I rock it, sing lullabies.

In time the pram rests peacefully
for the childless one,
the emptied one,
the one who kept on seeing
wrapped around her bed
red aprons.

PAT BORTHWICK

Love Song
for my husband

This dead baby you gave me
dragged in a sack
banging against my legs
tripping me up

I hate you

This dead baby
I hate what you cannot give me

This dead baby
carried around my neck
a rock
a stone
a hollow bone
clanking against my breast

First sight you said
You loved me just like that
No doubts
    not once
And I seduced accepted it

Now 8 years on and longing
no baby
only a dead metaphor
falling
      between us
rocking the stone bed of our meaning

Waking at night beside you
watching the soft curve of your lip
wanting my baby to have it
and knowing nothing can come of it

No meaning between us
except what we create
of touch
of stone
of hollow bone

Dead babies aching against my breast
rocking my hip
feeling myself
belly-full of it

Nothing is left of lust
but loving the air between us
creating some new meanings
    out of nothingness

BARBARA ZANDITON

from **Three Women**

SECOND VOICE:

When I first saw it, the small red seep, I did not believe it.

I watched the men walk about me in the office. They were so flat!

There was something about them like cardboard, and now I had caught it,

That flat, flat, flatness from which ideas, destructions,
Bulldozers, guillotines, white chambers of shrieks proceed,
Endlessly proceed – and the cold angels, the abstractions.
I sat at my desk in my stockings, my high heels,

And the man I work for laughed: 'Have you seen something
  awful?
You are so white, suddenly.' And I said nothing.
I saw death in the bare trees, a deprivation.
I could not believe it. Is it so difficult
For the spirit to conceive a face, a mouth?
The letters proceed from these black keys, and these black keys
  proceed
From my alphabetical fingers, ordering parts,

Parts, bits, cogs, the shining multiples.
I am dying as I sit. I lose a dimension.
Trains roar in my ears, depatures, departures!
The silver track of time empties into the distance,
The white sky empties of its promise, like a cup.
These are my feet, these mechanical echoes.
Tap, tap, tap, steel pegs. I am found wanting.

SYLVIA PLATH

Decision

Child, I choose not to have you.

Unsure
what you bring, I quail
before your huge beginning.

Forgive me
I feel bright young birth blue
I am not ready.

I fear I will never be ready.

I would shower love upon you, but
my eyes just opening you will close
as clams around you, damn
my seas into a lake, lapping
calm and careful
on your changing shores.

Forgive me

I am not ready.

DOROTHY BAIRD

The Abortion

Somebody who should have been born is gone.

Just as the earth puckered its mouth,
each bud puffing out from its knot,
I changed my shoes, and then drove south.

Up past the Blue Mountains, where
Pennsylvania humps on endlessly,
wearing, like a crayonned hat, its green hair,

its roads sunken in like a grey washboard;
where, in truth, the ground cracks evilly,
a dark socket from which the coal has poured,

Somebody who should have been born is gone.

the grass as bristly and stout as chives,
and me wondering when the ground would break,
and me wondering how anything fragile survives;

up in Pennsylvania, I met a little man,
not Rumpelstiltskin, at all, at all . . .
he took the fullness that love began.

Returning north, even the sky grew thin
like a high window looking nowhere.
The road was as flat as a sheet of tin,

Somebody who should have been born is gone.

Yes, woman, such logic will lead
to loss without death. Or say what you meant,
you coward . . . this baby that I bleed.

ANNE SEXTON

She promises her firstborn daughters to the religious life if God will allow her to survive a dangerous miscarriage
(Galway, 1903)

'Blood is bulging now
like a field drain
between my thighs.
I am leaching away
I am muck in a downpour.
O Christ make haste to help me.

I offer them up
doves in a cage of love
doves for your temple.
I fumble to grasp your hem
as a dam
a falling sluicegate
as a twist of rag merely
to stopper the neck
my life is leaking through.

This is a bargain clearly
a clenching of need.
I bind my daughters now
to perpetual love.
May they rest
in a peace beyond recall
sealed wells
in a yard enclosed.

I must live as a vessel
a vessel only.
Sure and to God
some day I'll bear him
his living son.'

CATHERINE BYRON

The Lost Baby Poem

the time i dropped your almost body down
down to meet the waters under the city
and run one with the sewage to the sea
what did i know about waters rushing back
what did i know about drowning
or being drowned

you would have been born into winter
in the year of the disconnected gas
and no car   we would have made the thin
walk over Genesee hill into the Canada wind
to watch you slip like ice into strangers' hands
you would have fallen naked as snow into winter
if you were here i could tell you these
and some other things

if i am ever less than a mountain
for your definite brothers and sisters
let the rivers pour over my head
let the sea take me for a spiller
of seas   let black men call me stranger
always   for your never named sake

LUCILLE CLIFTON

For You, Who Didn't Know

At four a.m. I dreamed myself on that beach
where we'll take you after you're born
I woke in a wave of blood.

Lying in the backseat of a nervous Chevy
I counted the traffic lights, lonely as planets.
Starlings stirred in the robes of Justice

over the Town Hall. Miscarriage of justice,
they sang, while you, my small client
went curling away like smoke under my ribs.

Kick me! I pleaded. Give me a sign
that you're still there!
Train tracks shook our flesh from our bones.

Behind the hospital rose a tree of heaven.
>   *You can learn something from everything*
>   a rabbi told his hasidim who did not believe it.
>   I didn't believe it either, O rabbi,
>   what did you learn on the train to Belsen.
>   *That because of one second one can miss everything.*

There are rooms on this earth for emergencies.
A sleepy attendant steals my clothes and my name,
and leaves me among the sinks on an altar of fear.
'Your name. Your name. Sign these papers,
authorising us in our wisdom to save the child.
Sign here for circumcision. Your faith, your faith.'

O rabbi, what can we learn from the telegraph?
asked the hasidim, who did not understand.
And he answered, *That every word is counted and charged.*

'This is called a dobtone,' smiles the doctor.
He greases my belly, stretched like a drum
and plants a microphone there, like a flag.

A thousand thumping rabbits! Savages clapping for joy!
A heart dancing its name, I'm here, I'm here!
The cries of fishes, of stars, the tunings of hair!

O rabbi, what can we learn from a telephone?
My schicksa daughter, your faith, your faith
that what we say here is heard there.

NANCY WILLARD

To My Unborn Daughter

Ursula little bear you are
distant as the stars
close as the beat of my blood.
I feel you butt against
my bowels, I can chart
your travels, track you
as I would a star's spoor
light years away under
my palm. We will meet
soon, waylayer of my
plans, wanderer in
my forest: and I can
tell you I'm scared.
Sing to me now
from the depths
which hatched you,
sing across the
great divide, sing me

strong and I will paw
the ground and roar
the sky down. And so
the grizzly will find
her cub, the star will
bury its head in earth,
we shall yelp and frolic
and pretend we knew
it all along.

LESLEY SAUNDERS

Home
for my unborn child

Home
is a series of memories
strung like tendons through time
holding the heart in place.

Home
remembers in the bones.

Home
is the marrow
making the white blood cells
fighting off the abscess
of despair.

Home
holds my hands
helping itself more generously
to my heart
than it has any right to.

Home
is a place
less tenuous than scent.

tonight
thinking of you
making a home
making a place for your heart
to come home to
creating a space where your memories
will cling as sturdy as weeds
amidst the debris of our lives
I anticipate your touch
the scent of your skin
as strongly as memory
awaiting your birth
and making a home
for you to cling to
and flee from.

BARBARA ZANDITON

Tempo

In the first month I think
it's a drop in a spider web's
necklace of dew

at the second a hazel-nut; after,
a slim Black-eyed Susan demurely folded
asleep on a cloudy day

then a bush-baby silent as sap
in a jacaranda tree, but blinking
with mischief

at five months it's an almost-caught
flounder flapping back
to the glorious water

six, it's a song
with a chorus of basses; seven, five grapefruit
in a mesh bag that bounces on the hip
on a hot morning down at the shops

a water-melon next – green oval
of pink flesh and black seeds, ripe
waiting to be split by the knife

nine months it goes faster, it's a bicycle
pedalling for life over paddocks
of sun
no, a money-box filled with silver half-crowns
a sunflower following the clock
with its wide-open grin
a storm in the mountains, spinning rocks
down to the beech trees
three hundred feet below
– old outrageous Queen Bess's best dress
starched ruff and opulent tent of a skirt
packed with ruffles and lace
no no, I've remembered, it's a map
of intricate distinctions
purples for high ground burnt umber
for foothills green for the plains
and the staggering blue beyond
waiting and waiting and
aching
with waiting

no more alternatives! Suddenly now
you can see my small bag of eternity
pattern of power
my ace of adventure
my sweet-smelling atom
my planet, my grain of miraculous dust
my green leaf, my feather
my lily, my lark
look at her angels –
this is my daughter.

LAURIS EDMOND

LABOUR
The Way Out Is Through Fire

Poem to Ease Birth

In the house with the tortoise chair
    she will give birth to the pearl
        to the beautiful feather

in the house of the goddess who sits on a tortoise
    she will give birth to the necklace of pearls
        to the beautiful feathers we are

there she sits on the tortoise
    swelling to give us birth

on your way on your way
    child be on your way to me here
        you whom I made new

come here child   come be pearl
        be beautiful feather

ANON *(from Nahuatl, Aztec, translated by A. Hello)*

from Three Poems of Incarnation

I INVOCATION
At the day's end I found

Nightfall wrapped about a stone.

I took the cold stone in my hand,
The shadowy surfaces of life unwound,
And within I found
A bird's fine bone.

I warmed the relic in my hand
Until a living heart
Beat, and the tides flowed
Above, below, within.

There came a boat riding the storm of blood
And in the boat a child,

In the boat a child
Riding the waves of song,
Riding the waves of pain.

II INVOCATION
Child in the little boat
Come to the land
Child of the seals
Calf of the whale
Spawn of the octopus
Fledgling of cormorant
Gannet and herring-gull,
Come from the sea,
Child of the sun,
Son of the sky.

Safely pass
The mouths of the water,
The mouths of night,
The teeth of the rocks,
The mouths of the wind,
Safely float
On the dangerous waves
Of an ocean sounding
Deeper than red
Darker than violet,
Safely cross
The ground-swell of pain
Of the waves that break
On the shores of the world.

Life everlasting
Love has prepared
The paths of your coming.
Plankton and nekton
Free-swimming pelagic
Spawn of the waters

Has brought you to birth
In the life-giving pools,
Spring has led you
Over the meadows
In fox's fur
Has nestled and warmed you,
With the houseless hare
In the rushes has sheltered
Warm under feathers
Of brooding wings
Safe has hidden
In the grass secretly
Clothed in disguise
Of beetle and grasshopper
Small has laid you
Under a stone
In the nest of the ants
Myriadfold scattered
In pollen of pine forests
Set you afloat
Like dust on the air
And winged in multitudes
Hatched by the sun
From the mud of rivers.

Newborn you have lain
In the arms of mothers,
You have drawn life
From a myriad breasts,
The mating of animals
Has not appalled you,
The longing of lovers
You have not betrayed,
You have come unscathed
From the field of battle
From famine and plague
You have lived undefiled
In the gutters of cities
We have seen you dancing
Barefoot in villages

You have been to school.
But kept your wisdom.

Child in the little boat,
Come to the land,
Child of the seals.

KATHLEEN RAINE

Dream-Drumming

I braced the drum to my arm, a flat drum, and began to play.
He heard me and she heard me. I had never seen this drum
   before.
As I played, weakness went through me; weakness left me.
   I held my arms high, the drum and the soft-headed long
      stick
I drummed past my tiredness vibrating weakness, past it into
   music,
As in ragas past exhaustion into the country of all music.

Held my arms high, became that vibration, drummed the
   sacrifice of my belly.
He heard me, she heard me,
I turned into the infinity figure, reaching down into the earth
   of music with my legs at last,
Reaching up from the two circles, my pelvic sea,
   mountains and air of breast, with my arms up into music
At last turned into music, drumming on that possessed
   vibration,
Drumming my dream.

MURIEL RUKEYSER

The New Door

The labour of two men
to break open a wall
takes several days. They sweat,
ache, the heat denies them
shade; for a skilled worker's rate
their hands sting with the baking, rough
surface of the wall.
It is a journey they make. Practical
as explorers, they plot the route.
Layer after layer of bricks
come loose. One brick
after another and the day is solid,
the destination assured, everything
lies in the feel of the bricks
prised out, passed hand to hand,
laid down.
Enough for them now to be pushing
through the wall, dismantling its resistance,
its silent and obstinate passivity.
Once through
that will be the past
for them, for ever: the future,
another journey.

Only the new door,
for ever between *there*
and *here*, swinging
again and again between them
and its frame, touching at both flanks
each raw-edged brick, survivor,
commands the process,
knowledge,
they unknowingly began.

PIPPA LITTLE

Labour Pains

I am sick today,
sick in my body,
eyes wide open, silent,
I lie on the bed of childbirth.

Why do I,
so used to the nearness of death,
To pain and blood and screaming . . .
now uncontrollably tremble with dread?

A nice young doctor tried to comfort me,
and talked about the joy of giving birth.
Since I know better than he about this matter,
What good purpose can his prattle serve?

Knowledge is not reality.
Experience belongs to the past.
Let those who lack immediacy be silent.
Let observers be content to observe.

I am all alone,
totally, utterly, entirely on my own,
gnawing my lips, holding my body rigid,
waiting on inexorable fate.

There is only one truth.
I shall give birth to a child,
truth driving outward from my inwardness.
Neither good nor bad; real, no sham about it.

With the first labour pains,
suddenly the sun goes pale.
The indifferent world goes strangely calm.
I am alone.
It is alone I am.

*YOSANO AKIKO (translated from Japanese by K. Rexroth
and I. Atsumi)*

Threshold

My mother, saying only
This is for when your time comes,
gave me a stick of wood, scarred
by the marks of teeth.

She made no explanation
but touched me at breast and waist.
I did not tell her that my moon-blood
had ceased to flow; nor did I ask

the wise woman when my belly waxed
why that should be, though I feared
the movements within, and my steps
grew slow with the weight I bore.

When the angry rippling began to surge
through and through my flesh the women
led me to the valley that was no man's.
Pitiless tides possessed me.

The stubborn wood that my mother's teeth
had bruised was in my mouth.
I strove against it, biting hard,
and the grain held.

Still I did not know for how long
the pain might last, how fierce its peak
nor its purpose. Clasping the women's hands,
groaning against the clenched wood,

I thrust as if to cast out death. But life
slid from me onto the spread rushes,
a new mouth cried out. The wooden talisman
is my trust for this child when she grows.

And she shall have more:
my careful words against fear.

PAMELA GILLILAN

from **Three Women**

FIRST VOICE:
I am calm. I am calm. It is the calm before something awful:
The yellow minute before the wind walks, when the leaves
Turn up their hands, their pallors. It is so quiet here.
The sheets, the faces, are white and stopped, like clocks.
Voices stand back and flatten. Their visible hieroglyphs
Flatten to parchment screens to keep the wind off.
They paint such secrets in Arabic, Chinese!

I am dumb and brown. I am a seed about to break.
The brownness is my dead self, and it is sullen:
It does not wish to be more, or different.
Dusk hoods me in blue now, like a Mary.
O colour of distance and forgetfulness! —
When will it be, the second when Time breaks
And eternity engulfs it, and I drown utterly?

I talk to myself, myself only, set apart —
Swabbed and lurid with disinfectants, sacrificial.
Waiting lies heavy on my lids. It lies like sleep,
Like a big sea. Far off, far off, I feel the first wave tug
Its cargo of agony toward me, inescapable, tidal.
And I, a shell, echoing on this white beach
Face the voices that overwhelm, the terrible element.

*   *   *

There is no miracle more cruel than this.
I am dragged by the horses, the iron hooves.
I last. I last it out. I accomplish a work.
Dark tunnel, through which hurtle the visitations,
The visitations, the manifestations, the startled faces.
I am the center of an atrocity.
What pains, what sorrows must I be mothering?

Can such innocence kill and kill? It milks my life.
The trees wither in the street. The rain is corrosive.
I taste it on my tongue, and the workable horrors,
The horrors that stand and idle, the slighted godmothers

With their hearts that tick and tick, with their satchels of
    instruments.
I shall be a wall and a roof, protecting.
I shall be a sky and a hill of good: O let me be!

A power is growing on me, an old tenacity.
I am breaking apart like the world. There is this blackness,
This ram of blackness. I fold my hands on a mountain.
The air is thick. It is thick with this working.
I am used. I am drummed into use.
My eyes are squeezed by this blackness.
I see nothing.

SYLVIA PLATH

Caesarean

Look. Those are my pelvic bones
hanging on the wall beyond the bed
black and white nut-crackers
could trap a tunnelling head.

What time is it
What time is it?
Midnight. I feel gigantic, I quake
with synthetic labour
an oyster bulging with its pearl.

Yes. I'll sign the forms.
Please drain my stomach
with plastic tubes; I agree.

Someone draws a careful line
on drum-tight skin.
That is the opening place.

Rubber hands, sterile hands,
Whose hands?
salvage my son.
The knifed womb sleeps.

My mouth wakes, my lips
are numb. I must praise
his sleek uncrumpled skull.
Amazing! Here's a conjuror's coin
spun from a fool in the dark.

When I close my eyes
he will roll away
down chattering corridors.

Daylight. I can smell chrysanthemums.
Everything is definite and shiny.
Nurse, my neat cosmetic scar
is itching.

I am drowsy, almost dreaming.
Where is he?
I don't want to dream again
of monstrous other truer births
in glassy caves of pain.

HERMIONE HUXLEY

The Crossing

All night the sea tossed me
like egg yolk in a basin
and rocked the baby in my belly

So here, arriving
it is not I, but we
all churned up and frothing
with still, at the window
the sea of our crossing

Milky, simmering
she laps at our door
while I'm lying in water,
drowning, distraught

Even in the bath
I'm assailed by kicks
the vicious struggle
of an ugly chick

I lie fearful at night
while rain, wind and sea
puncture the fine membrane of the house

and the child inside
rolls like an eyeball
beneath skin grown fine as an eyelid

JILL DAWSON

Witholding
(remembered fragment of a burnt poem)

. . . A secret unshared
Is a crying voice in the wilderness;
Seeking an ear
With the intensity of a lost soul.
It is a birth impeded,
Annunciation gagged,
A pent-up river
Ripping at its barricades.

Oh for a needlepoint
To pierce the caul
In which the child is wrapped,
To give him utterance;
To let his birthcry fall upon glad ears
For whom his advent

And his vigour
And his advocacy
Are wholly welcome joy.

STELLA WHITING

Birth 16 ix 78

1 The pod of my flesh
bulged and split
unwilling
to shed its fruit.
The doctor yelled
Get out at my lover
and my friend who
held my hand.
I wanted her
to be kind.
Catheters were
inserted and
a rubber mask
went over my face.
They pierced my waters
with a pin.
We waited.
I watched for dawn.
Only waiting
in bright light,
the clink of trolleys
and smell
of germicide.
He was born
oh yes
as I lay draped
in a green gown
feet in the air
feeling nothing,
he was born.

II I'm crying now
for that pain.
Scarred, I will
never heal:
the skin on my belly
wrinkled with sudden age
my vulva stitched and raw
tits swollen and dripping.
Scared of dying.
He lay in a metal cot
with a tube in his nose
and his father cried.
I shall go on crying
until this birth is expiated.

The child sucks at me
unerringly, without
gratitude.

I shall go on crying
until this birth
is expiated.

LESLEY SAUNDERS

Serenade for Strings
(for Peter)

I At nine from behind the door
The tap tapping
Is furtive, insistent:
Recurrent, imperative
The I AM crying
Exhorting, compelling.

At eleven louder!
Wilderness shaking
Boulders uprolling
Mountains creating

And deep in the cavern
No longer the hammer
Faintly insistent
No longer the pickaxe
Desperate to save us
But minute by minute
The terrible knocking
God at the threshold!
Knocking down darkness
Battering daylight.

II   *O green field*
O sun soaked
On lavish emerald
Blade and sharp bud piercing
O green field
Cover and possess me
Shield me in brightness now
From the knocking
The terrible knocking. . . .

III   Again . . . Again . . . O again,
Midnight. A new day.
Day of days
Night of nights
Lord of lords.

Good Lord deliver us
Deliver us of the new lord
Too proud for prison
Too urgent for the grave . . .
Deliver us, deliver us.

    O God the knocking
    The knocking attacking
    No breath to fight it
    No thought to bridge it
    Bare body wracked and writhing
    Hammered and hollowed
    To airless heaving.

IV   The clock now. Morning.
Morning come creeping
Scrublady slishing
And sloshing the waxway
And crying O world
Come clean
Clean for the newborn
The sun soon rising . . .

Rising and soaring
On into high gear . . .
Sudden knowledge!
Easy speedway
Open country
Hills low-flying
Birds up-brooding
Clouds caressing
A burning noon-day . . .

Now double wing-beat
Breasting body
Till cloudways open
Heaven trembles:
   And blinding
     searing
       terrifying
         cry!

The final bolt has fallen,
The firmament is riven.

V   *Now it is done.*
Relax. Release.
And here, behold your handiwork:
Behold – a man!

DOROTHY LIVESAY

The Midwife

Walking amid the flames of hell,
listening to the howls of the damned,
she feels at home
in hell.

Inflicting pain,
stroking the sweat-matted hair.
Saying little. Shouting.

Her awesomely clean hands
are wise and sad
like God.

ANNA SWIR

Oxytocin

The electric pump clicks.
Drip fed through that meter,
by clear plastic tubes
and a needle jammed into my vein,
this is not my body's pain.

It did not rise like breath
or the fierce arched rainbows
I have imagined.

From a burning bush,
it spreads a forest fire,
with me in front of it,
running.

SUSAN TAYLOR

Notes from the Delivery Room

Strapped down,
victim in an old comic book,
I have been here before,
this place where pain winces
off the walls
like too bright light.
Bear down a doctor says,
foreman to sweating labourer
but this work, this forcing
of one life from another
is something that I signed for
at a moment when I would have signed anything.
Babies should grow in fields;
common as beets or turnips
they should be picked and held
not end up, soil spilling
from between their toes –
and how much easier it would be later,
returning them to earth.
Bear up . . . bear down . . . the audience
grows restive, and I'm a new magician
who can't produce the rabbit
from my swollen hat.
She's crowning, someone says,
but there is no one royal here,
just me, quite barefoot,
greeting my barefoot child.

LINDA PASTAN

Open Wide

Concentrating faces grouped themselves
Around us at the operating table.
'Choose a mask,' the anaesthetist had said,
Showing his shiny 'space gas' machine.
My son, an innocent play-mate
Put the black rubber on,
And smiled whilst playing with the tubes.
'No need to hold him down,' the same man said –
As hands and arms clutched
Suddenly in panic, my son's
Face changed to fear.
The game had too.

Tears came simultaneously.
I laid my head on his front,
As he had done when born.
Only I had held the mask then,
Clinging to a life-line, a
Hissing pipe that took the
Noise of pain away.
And when I'd finally lain down,
(Upright to the end), I writhed
Ecstatically to see in a
Mirror they held, the climax
Of this act of love.

So, who gave birth to who then?
And, who is the mother now?
I wept and missed my child today
Like I was the longing one.
He only remembered the bump
That brought him down to earth;
Now, safely landed too, I disconnect
The twisted cords and umbilical bonds,
Cut and mend old birth scars, feel
Breasts no longer aching to feed.
My body is my own again and
The after glow of giving birth
Puts life back into me.

What I won't forget is
You nearly died – was it

                    separation shock?
When they laid you down you
Forgot to breathe – I held
Mine till you choked back to life.
Now I'm the one to give you its kiss
Not smother you with lies.

Both our masks have gone now.
We play this game apart.

VALERIE DENTON

The Last Word

On the lighted page
Veins are dark under stretched skin.
Look where the flesh is torn
Yet pulls together and heals.
Most of the pages are filled;
The veins stretch, covering another.
A tide filling a beach,
Blossom firming into fruit –
Who can halt a full-term womb?
The book burns brightly, blurs the background;
Unspeaking watchers have stood for a long time
In the darkness; they see with inherited eyes.
The silence is that of fired ground
When the harvest has been gathered
And the stubble burnt off.
Now the great dumbness leans trembling forward
To the delivery.
Sharp as a birth cry,
From the words the white breath comes
Scorching scalding every black shadow
And those who lurk in them.
It hovers over those watchers

Who for so long stood by the book.
Now the last word rises from the open flesh,
Ripping itself free of the cord.
Like a terrible god the word
Advances,
Armed with a beauty that kills
Or gives life back.

JOAN BOARD

The Gift

I laboured long
for another's brainchild
while my own lay
stilled
my sweat spent
on another's vision
my own dream quenched
and smoking.
My soul is garnering
a late harvest
finds no field
to spread its ripeness.

Surprised by slow fire
simmering the bones
in the drowsing hours
my thoughts stab
in mute rebellion
commence
the relentless search
to be born
the longing of matter
to receive form.

My imagination
as bits of coloured glass
wayward children
many shapes and shades
that will not come back
when I call –
go running
in a thousand directions;
the mind a filter
determining the day's colour
but feelings run riot
like leaves in an autumn yard.

I am all gathered up
and hunger has taken me
the ferment of long-trodden grapes
is the fume that stokes the furnace.
Now fear has lost me
I sing out my heart
as some plantation slave
with the pungent smell of freedom
rolling, echoing the notes out
with power, resonance, hope.

ROSEMARY PALMEIRA

The Way Out

The way out is through fire,
a burning stairway
three doors like sentries.

the last but one
child from another time
steadies herself to brave it

then slight and calm
darts into the burning.
Her courage cannot save her –

a haze of blue flames etch
their mad dance
that draws her like wind

waves of heat curl hissing
and scarlet break on her calves
she cries out with pain

as she passes through the first door
and labours upward
where soundless as the sun

the white fire
folds her to its breast.
Her breath sighs from her now

like dying leaves
as scorched and fainting she meets
the second door heavy as a vault

and passes through it
and climbs unfaltering
into the dark invisible heart of fire.

The last door
glows with angel heat, molten
immovable.

She flings her frail weight
against it
as it bites away her hands.

I remember a bird, nest aflame
its wings alight
circling higher and higher

into a black tar of smoke
like a beating star
circling and rising as its light

grew brighter and unbearably
brighter
towards a doorway that must open

a hand cool as rain
outstretch
at the height of heaven.

The way out is never so bitter
never so bitter.
Perhaps it is through water.

JENI COUZYN

For Marion

i am calling to the child
thru the knot in my stomach
i am calling to the child
thru the seaweed
thru the stone on the beach
thru the grain of sand
thru the baby's hair
thru the ebb and flow of tide

i am rubbing my stomach
in the child
in the sand
in the spark of light
in the water

you are in the air, child
in the healing hands
of an old woman
child-in-the-spark-of
her blue eyes

The Way Out is through Fire

she says   let the birth come
            in your hands
            in your shoulders
            in your head
            let the child come
            into all your heart centers

JUDITH BOLLINGER

BIRTH

Aloud Into The Light

The Birth of Vahakri

The skies were in labour
and the muscles of the earth
and the ripe red seas were in labour.
And in labour too the reeds of the shore.
And out of one small red reed, smoke.
And out of the smoke, flames.
And out of the yellow flames of the reed
a blond boy ran,
with flickering fire hair,
and a beard of live fire.
And his eyes were two suns.

ANON (translated from Ancient Armenian)

To Enter that Rhythm Where the Self is Lost

To enter that rhythm where the self is lost,
where breathing: heartbeat: and the subtle music
of their relation make our dance, and hasten
us to the moment when all things become
magic, another possibility.
That blind moment, midnight, when all sight
begins, and the dance itself is all our breath,
and we ourselves the moment of life and death.
Blinded;   but given now another saving,
the self as vision, at all times perceiving,
all arts all senses being languages,
delivered of will, being transformed in truth –
for life's sake surrendering moment and images,
writing the poem;   in love making;   bringing to birth.

MURIEL RUKEYSER

Lazarus

It was the amazing white, it was the way he simply
Refused to answer our questions, it was the cold pale glance
Of death upon him, the smell of death that truly
Declared his rising to us. It was no chance
Happening, as a man may fill a silence
Between two heart-beats, seem to be dead and then
Astonish us with the closeness of his presence;
This man was dead, I say it again and again.
All of our sweating bodies moved towards him
And our minds moved too, hungry for famished faith.
He would not enter our world at once with words
That we might be tempted to twist or argue with:
Cold like a white root pressed in the bowels of earth
He looked, but also vulnerable – like birth.

ELIZABETH JENNINGS

Birthday

There is a tree outside the window.
It is to make them believe they are
in the country for a holiday.
Moonlight, it is two in the morning,
Time of the body's least resistance.

A venetian blind forms the bars of
The prison of responsibility
For the children of their loving nights
And days. The children of their loving.

The red warning light,
The red warning blood
That drips steadily
From the slowly
Exploding body.

One too slow for them
Cut – her tearing flesh
Damns her consciousness.

He is blue with rage.
He, raging because
She was too slow in helping him into
The bright world he wanted so badly
Here is her slow son.
But where is her love?

Where are the men when the women are called?
When the huge body is out of control,
And the so-called pain is really waves of
Anguished loneliness as though the real
Truth had finally dawned and was more difficult
To bear than the slowest child. The huge truth
That she is alone, and forever.

And the silence of women
After the birth
Is fear.

EVELYN PASCAL GRUNDY

The Birth

Longer ago than leaps my mind
I, not I, a younger older wiser me
welled with the world
a softness, strong in woman, all
feeling full with being, a gown
of dusk down blurring, holding
healing in my heart, was round womb, wound
with seasons, wise with moon
with whom I shared my tidal seas,
sleeping while her eye was open.

I was the world was me. We rolled in
darkness down together, deep
drunk with being; until he grew,
a grumble in my depths at first, and grew,
a grit that gathered snow,
ice-cold and calling sounds
that wounded me, until too heavy –
heaped in me he lay; and long I laboured
pressing him, his icy wind,
aloud into the light.

He was my son, this hard and separated form,
that left me seeking light; my night
would smother him, he said, seeing nothing
with my eyes, but sure that his were true.

Alone I live in shadows shoring up his dreams
and wait with all my woman wealth
until his dawn delves in my sea, and thaws
his ice-bound thought. Then soft and hard
will lace with love; his lips of light
will call my name, and all my moon warmed might
will wave into his word, and heal the hurt
of cloven hearts; the world will hear our gasp
– of oneness in our birth.

DOROTHY BAIRD

Birth Stories

I get high on birth stories
the way other people get high over a pint
or watching a good film.
The kind of stories most people would rather not hear about –
36 hours in labour, haemorrhaged,
had third degree tears, stitched up in catgut.

I long for the importance of it,
as if it's an obstacle course I have to run
before I can call myself WOMAN.

I crave the whole experience, even painful haemorroids.
Myself, protuberant, heels on toilet seat, suffering.
'LORD, THOU ART HARD ON MOTHERS
WE SUFFER IN THEIR COMING AND THEIR GOING'
Lord, we suffer if they don't come at all.

A baby, soft and ripe as a blackberry,
with goosedown for hair and a warm little laugh.

But then I remember, the days of my pregnancy,
and how suddenly, the two-roomed flat became my prison.
time became telescoped into the next seven months.

I did not believe my own dreams of bliss and maternity.
I saw rather, a baby, raw with hunger and cold.
I saw my own failure.

For £140 I cancelled the possibility
of the blue-eyed son I knew I was carrying.
A weekend in a private clinic in Chiswick,
it was clean and relatively painless.
A nurse from Clare brought me tea
and said I'd be back again, most likely.
'Ah', she sighed, 'the convent nuns!'
I cried, and craved the pain I should have felt,
and the pain I still feel,
but can't locate
except in birth stories.

GER DUFFY

Labour Day
(for Christopher)

The nighties were in the case in their shop folds
And the soap, not the kind for everydays,
And the thin clothes, for afterwards.

Sister took the case.
She turned her width and bristly neck to face me.
   'Pop out of your things and pop into bed.
   Brave girls don't cry in my ward.
   No husbands here – the only place you're safe
   From bloody men.'

She laughed a midwife's laugh,
Thick with birth jokes, coated with the dirt of centuries.

   'And doctor does not wish to see hair rollers –
   Remember manners ladies.'

The other two women were regulars.
One cried a lot; she and Stan hadn't intended this.

And there was a Catholic behind a Woodbine screen
In for the 5th.
   '*His* last sin' she said.

In a day they became again the stooped backs,
The used bodies, bellying over new babies,
Dowdy cows mooing together
Awaiting the milking.

I went home with you
Stopping off at a cafe
To delay the real beginning.

I forgot you, and had to go back
To lift the carrycot off the table stained with tea.

I wiped the cot down.

It was new –
A present, you see.

ANGELA COOKE

On Birth

No help, not the battalions
Of facts and probabilities
Trained to snort out terror
Where it squats –

Leave me my fear, it comes
Low-lying, holy in the blood
And pours an angel's language
Through my heart;

Not my language, I will trust
This travelled wisdom, as
Books break on my brain,
On its gristled edges;

And I cannot understand you,
Or dream that I do,
Far asleep and sealed up
In the dangled dark.

LANNY KENNISH

Birth

He lies scarlet in my lap
An unexploded shell
Eyes blind from raging cries
Fingers clawing at the air
Like tiny crustaceans
Until his passion
Hoarse and powerful as a blow-torch
Moves his mouth even in sleep
As in an imprecation

This was a strange and difficult birth

ELIZABETH TEMPLE

Christmas Baby

Stab sudden, severe, shaft-in-spine.
Ease past the holly. Gasp. No sure sign.
Yet near the date – and pain, pain, dull in veins
That peaks to spikes, breath-fraught, until it wanes:
Strong as the hard gloss sheen to shed, to hold no more –
Holly, black cruel holly in my head, but for
A berry-whole, berry-bright child. Mine.

ANGELA BROWN

Two Daughters from the Myrtle Grove[1]

My first daughter
was a late, late twin,
pirate lover in a scallop shell.
She mowed me down.
I lodged rivalry
in the dampening earth.

1. The myrtle is a symbol of fertility.

The first child proves
treacherous the madonna's eye,
she tears off recalcitrant skins,
calls up the tall fountain
of lost mothers,
softens proud bone.

The second child
trowels the lazy mother soil.
And born of this second child,
she lifts the loose latch.
Drinking from Bede's wood,[2]
I soak now in wise water.

Glimpsing the border
I let the first girl go,
see crystal in the human rhyme,
cool custodian to this new totem.
And taut as gut I bear
on two-cross slabs of stone[3]

The second daughter,
long skull pushing all flesh
pitiless and raw.
She loops seas over scudding land,
takes all honour for her raft.
A fierce trembling. And out.

KAY SYRAD

2. An old oak chair in St Paul's, Jarrow, thought to have belonged to the Venerable Bede. Pregnant women drank water in which fragments of the chair had been soaked, for pain-free childbirth.
3. The Teampull-Na-mBan, or 'woman's church', on the island of Inishmurray, off the west coast of Ireland, has two cross-slabs outside on to which labouring women held, to ease the pain of childbirth.

After Birth

A rich red seaweed,
Rope-like and ragged, riveting as
Offal floated in the bath:
Membrane, that once flushed
Future into my baby, my son,
Now spent as a burst balloon.

Your miraculous
Conception escalated to a
Bloody birth. At our meeting
I cried while you shrieked;
My delight was your catastrophe.
Consummate rose limbs threshed in
Terror shocking space
As you awoke to my world. I lay
Gashed and gasping, transfixed with
Needles and wonder,
As you lay in the scales. Later came

Night, elongated by pain –
Branded and branded
Again and again. Bleeding. Aching.
Barred from turning by pain. Mean
Relief in brief sleep.
At five o'clock you were wheeled in, a
Hungry gift: forget-me-not
Blue eyes, chastened face,
Inkling body blanketed bud-tight.
Timidly you took my breast,
Drawing on our bond.

We awoke together. Behind us
Labour's mangle: those hours,
Deep and raw, rollered
Out all vanity of mortal force.

The first peelings of my womb
Were stirred now round the
Bath. The first fruit had fallen ripely,
Bursting life juice as he came.

SALLY SERVIAN

Transformation

I see you dart into the world
pearly pink like the inside of a shell
streaked with silver.

Look! Look!
I am shouting with joy, rising up
like a phoenix from my pain

With my eyes I behold you
In the flesh I behold you

So a holy man waking into death
from a life of devotion or
martyrdom in flames

might look into the shining face of god
and see at once
he had never believed.

I see you with my eyes
I see you in glory.

From a tatter of flesh I watch them work.
From a pinnacle of joy.
The placenta, purplish liver meat

sails out of my body like a whale
rubbery hands turn it inside out
hold it up to the light.

The sinewy pulsing cord.
In a haze of peace they cut and stitch
my threaded body like scarlet linen

the midwife chatting comfortably
seated at her work, the needle threaded,
the thimble, the green thread

in and out, in and out.
Then washed and trim in clean sheets
they leave us: mother father child

three folded together.
I see your sleeping face
eyelids crescent lines, lips curled translucent

in stillness like a cowrie shell
whirlpool of your hair. I see you breathe.
In a still pool the moon lies quiet.

JENI COUZYN

Beginning

Imagine yourself closed up in a room
dark, bland, staying constantly still
and alone, always alone
now, ever was and ever shall be:
a mere seed of yourself, not giving, not receiving,
and expecting nothing more than nothing –

And then:
        light
breaks
into the room, the first light you've ever known
        and swallows you whole

        the walls fall away, space
with its fabulous blue blossoming
flings out infinite arms to you,
and all things come skipping across still water
        towards you, amazed magnet,
        centre of the instantly knowable world.

And the unhoped-for Others are there,
distant magnets for their own worlds,
closer than they ever could've been
had you hoped them near.
The fruit you share among you
is almost too beautiful to devour.

CATE PARISH

Born, Again

I want for myself the regions
toward two dreams and dreamers
who have undressed
their longings.

There are no ceilings
no noticeable doors, no floors.
I'm in the spinning mist
and tired of waiting.

Fast ocean movement here
tenacious on my path I flow
among some planets
The air bites at nothing

as I pass.
I have a silent crew:
I bring things that will exist
and we climb ladders

in the wet of blood.
Definitive ambition
for these two coupled beings
of my choice.

I want for myself the regions
now with two dreams and dreamers.
I greet again
my limits.

TEODORA WEBER

The Voice of the Woman

An excerpt from 'The Crumbles' ('The Wasteland' rewritten): a poem for my brother and sons.

A hard coming we had of it, my mother & I
'You nearly killed me, being born'
                                        that burden
– that I was nearly the death of her –
                                        I carried, carry still
hard and bitter agony for us, like death, our death.
All births walk that edge
                    I was born, certainly,
here I am, living proof of it
                            but something died
because something always has to die
at nativities:
                    an old way of doing things
familiar patterns, the status quo   the written & unwritten
laws of men   their spoken & unspoken words . . .
The male urgency thrusts life on us and kills too
&, dying, forces us into life, the eternal
bereavement & regeneration.

You can't breathe down there; it is airless

In an old scrapbook amidst abdications
the child had drawn
ominous black clouds emanating
from the chimney of the conventional house,
There was no-one to heed the warnings
(the tribe was in some kind of danger)
Years later the suppressed anger exploded

On the phone she says: 'Your father is dying.'
You ask me afterwards: 'How did you feel?'
I said: 'I felt elation.'   It was not elation, that was the wrong word.
I felt suddenly I could breathe. My lungs emptied
I gave up smoking.

How late change always comes, causing regret
time wasted, old habits, as if one could have forseen
and forestalled
                          However late, it must be welcomed with courage
Once seen, we cannot retreat.

This demystifying of the old gods
in their houses & temples
                                    places of learning
has to be done
                    if we are to find voice.

Now I speak with a voice of thunder ominous
heralding rain   unafraid
my breath gags on no truths
At the beginning of this re-birth
I am almighty as Thor.

One day even the sea might rush in to reclaim the abandoned shore
as on days of high storm the girl used to believe it would
and as in nightmares the woman sees the high mountain of surf
roaring towards the house
the house built on stones starved of the flood.

It is time for another flood.

PAT V. T. WEST

Pilgrim Woman
(for Pamela Fenton Marshall, 1926–1983)

This is my map: a square of crumpled cloth,
the continents scratched with my fingernail.
Though far, far out between two worlds
I know where I'm going.

This interim of yellow, fetid dark, clenched
hands, the sweated pain of travelling –
this must be done with soon.

Don't comfort me
don't make me weak.
I need endurance now
to focus
my one deep eye, a red jet burning.
For this I concede confinement, torture.
If I lose resolve
I'll fall to the sea floor, die again
and again, breathe only sour water.

In answer I dream of my landfall,
my horizon-curved ledges
stone-warm to the warm skin of my hands and my feet:
a whole, brown-skinned and straight-backed land,
rivers of good, strong blood in me
singing from sun to moon.
Here my lost, uncharted years
hang, lambent fruit, deep
in blue trees of the interior.

I wake to want,
again, to wrench this caul, this blindness
from my hand, rise up and use
these wasting bones. Already I
have carved my footprints on the shore.
I want to press my feet deep inside those prints!
I want to shed
my old selves quietly,
emerge
emerald and shining,
jagged as a butterfly.

Don't touch me:
don't hold me back.
Instead
I step from my body's ship
on to the salty stones.

Safe,
delivered,
triumphant,
everything is before me.

PIPPA LITTLE

To the Goddess

No happy smiling girl, Goddess –
You knew, you knew and yet
You saw me surrender
Time and time again into the arms of God.
You knew the agony, the tears
That washed my eyes away –
The knife of pain
That gouged deeper, deeper
Until my guts were strewn
Over your own receiving earth;
My body, small and weak
Falling again into his arms
To be mocked and wounded by you.
Now slowly, my time comes
In this old land between the mountains
And the sea – and I finally
Surrender myself to you; Goddess.
The rain sweeps down
To wash your newest-born
My tears
Kept safe by you, for years
Now, released, and returning to their mother;
The moon and tides cautiously noting
The arrival of the new initiate,
Not welcoming yet –
The mystery is harder than that –
And God,
What of him?
He joins his hands with yours, surrounding me
Creating a rainbow round the sun

His the part I marvel at, as before –
The visible fusion of colours in the light
And to complete the circle.
Yours, the part
Running deep into the earth
And sea, and now, I know
I know at last that it is there, Mother –
And I ask you to swaddle and nourish
This infant woman – me.

CAROLE BRUCE

Floating

I had to pass forty
to learn it: look up at the brightness
and let the clenched self go.

Before, I was too narrow
not trusting the balance of will in my body
not to slip through the spaces
in the skin of the water
the stretched molecules
they swore would buoy me up.

At the sea's edge, turned dense with terror
of sliding into the dark without even screaming
like a stillborn.

Times, we all hear the wind
especially the black throat of the wind in winter
threatening to blow us out,
feel our bodies teased on high places

but I have a pact with salt water
remembering it close over me
so, once, I knew I was starfished somewhere
older than air, feeling the ocean
stroking my throat into trance

soldering rolled-up eyes to the back of my skull
filling me with warm salt
winning me back
                    and I clung
to the bubble, to come back to the brightness
to be repierced by breath.

Twenty years I spent rooted
in the middle of land, forgetting the time-scale
of elements, keeping track of the caul
my father was born with
that he never needed, his own blood drowned him.
But since metal stiffens
in my hair, and I sag
from the spine with the stretched
weight of guts. I can spread my arms wide
and wait for absorption.

We all know it must happen
as owl fledglings must somehow know
one day they will step off
into dark. Almost casually
one afternoon, between a yawn
and a tidal swallow, some sea
might take me down. And I wonder
if my old monkey reflex
does not have me cling too hard

if it might not even be
a grateful merging, like letting mind
and body slide
into the flow of sleep
after making love, that other tiny
melting at the edge
of time. Brightness must
suck its burnish from the underside,
twin richnesses we strut between
that wait only to fill us in.

CHRISTINE EVANS

The Silver Bridge

The child ran across the silver bridge,
across the river bridge, high and dangerous,
the same both ways, like a palindrome.

The child ran across the silver bridge
into smaller and thinner distance.
In its loose coat that flapped, it ran,
and its shadow skipped across the grey waters below.

In my hand I hold a key
that will not open the child's heart.
From the height of the bridge,
its thoughts reach out to me longingly.

The child has crossed the bridge.
It stands on the opposite bank, watching me.
The child's shadow is a sleek full blue.
The child has gone first, to clear the way for me.

Mournful and mild, I set my foot
on the silver bridge.
The bridge buckles, there is a shriek
of silver metals.

The first touch of my weight pulls
the bridge down. I fall, spiralling
down to the bony waters, the key in my hand.
The outrider, the child, watches me.
Our glances coincide in air, two curves meeting.
the child is expressionless.
I enter the water, amid pangs like a birth.

PENELOPE SHUTTLE

To Say Yes

To say
yes
the explosion of
leaf into
light

Some
things grow
over the edges of
explanation
and there is no
        reading between
the lines because there are no
longer any lines
and no more need for
reading.

to find this so
sudden in each other
is to find ourselves with a
shock and instantaneous
sunk in an ocean bigger
than our puddle
bound comprehension can take
in   or swept up
into an air with no
horizon.

there are no
coasts or foothills
here   nothing to
climb   nothing to
cling to or
hide behind

unless we choose
to be invisible not to be
known

so much
easier to stay
stranger with
everything to say and
nothing to learn

than to say
yes

than to say
we have been
waiting all our lives
for this un
winding of rooftop and
rafter of the tough
fabric and fabrication
we put on
out of the womb

but we can
not be satisfied with
less

not satisfied
with a cold and singular
hole in the dumb
earth for
each of us

when we might un
tomb each
other with
a word
bear
down   give
birth to a common
language

say

yes

MARG YEO

Poem on Midsummer's Day

now is the year's fullness; like
a pregnant bride
she swells in white: the may's
lace tent, the curdy soup-
plates of the elderflower, cow-
parsley frothing like the scum of jam, the
glossy braid and tassels of tall grass

the hill's crown curls with fern
and foxgloves where I lie – blue
views of sloping fields whose ragged seams
are hedgerows deep in green; dark oaks
are parasols for cows; wild honeysuckle
ties the bees in loops

the Mendips shake out lanes
like linen bands; I am born here
dazzled, in white dust, and I drop down
between long banks, the scarlet course of campion
to where sheep squeal, and twitch
their fat rumps at the shears' steel buzz

I am the day's child, I am the year's fruit
now, at last, I am sweetened by sun
after cold seasoning; I am held
in the summer's arms, on a bed of piled warm wool

MICHÈLE ROBERTS

Rebirth

Water flooded everywhere
dripping over the edges of the plate of the world.
Spring stream rushing, impetuous white hurly-burly.
Slow-winding, green-pooled, golden-leaved in autumn.
Cart-track, thick mud carved by wheels,
black bowls laced with ice, glistening in the winter light.

Those floods washed me to the sea,
where waves dragged at my peripheries,
tentacled to my skin,
ebbing me away to be dissolved
and respun in the whirlpools of time.

I was laid bare to the bone of my spool.
I was harrowed –
the lines of the harrow drawn through my flesh;
the red blood pulsing,
repulsing,
the slivers of flesh sliced from the bone.
I was stripped and left naked.

I hung upside down in the womb
a second time,
hearing the thunder and surge
of water-distorted, body-absorbed voices
boom
beyond comprehension.

I longed for birth,
stretched out for understanding,
pushed through the new-found opening
at the base of the womb,
and fell, warm and confident
with many others through black space;
no limits known,
and filled with pleasure.

CATRIONA STAMP

NEWBORN
Still Soft Under Your Skin

Praise of a Child

A child is like a rare bird.
A child is precious like coral.
A child is precious like brass.
You cannot buy a child on the market.
Not for all the money in the world.
The child you can buy for money is a slave.
We may have twenty slaves, we may have thirty labourers,
Only a child brings us joy,
One's child is one's child.
The buttocks of our child are not so flat
That we should tie the beads on another child's hips.
One's child is one's child.
It may have a watery head or a square head,
One child is one's child.
It is better to leave behind a child,
Than let all the slaves inherit one's house.
One must not rejoice too soon over a child.
Only the one who is buried by his child,
Is the one who has truly borne a child.
On the day of our death, our hand cannot hold a single cowrie.
We need a child to inherit our belongings.

ANON *(from Yoruba, Nigeria, translated by U. Beier)*

The Damson

Where have you gone
small child
the damson bloom
on your eyes.

The still heap
of your flesh
lightly composed
in a grey shawl,
your skull's pulse

stains you,
the veins slip deep.

Two lights burn
at the mouth of the cave
where the air is thin
and the tunnels boom
with your slippery blood.

Your unripe cheeks cling
to the leaves, to the wall,
but your grasp unpeels
and your bruises murmur.

While blueness clouds
on the down of your eyes,
your tears erode
and your smile files

through your lips like a soldier
who shoots at the sky
and you flash up in silver;

Where are you now
little one,
peeled almond,
damson bloom?

HELEN DUNMORE

A New Kind of Fruit

It is a day for picking truth:
Ripe, within reach, fully rounded,
Tight skins hardly able to contain
For another day their readiness.

Once gathered, they can't be returned
To the stalk
Or barter resumed with the tree
However much the price agreed inflates.

Of course the fruit might have a sharpness
Requiring the palate to adjust
Or be accessible only
By catching it while you fall.

JOAN BOARD

Elation after Childbirth

I was not I. You were not me.
My love, papoose out of my thighs,
I rock you in huge cradles
Of my knees,
And I hear your first
Cry in darkness.

Now who am I?
Weeping through my hands
All weedy and yellow with
Dandelion nails and drunken fingers,
Blood tumbling through the
Folds of my footsteps
For this: flesh empty
And stomach all gone.

I wake and cannot find
You in myself, my arrow,
My blue-eyed Indian, my
New stick, my marrow,

My nude Indian
In your woollen blanket

On the ledge of the world.
My life. My phoenix-feather.

SANDRA HOCHMAN

Ciúnas

How I welcome you, little salmon
who leapt the womb, impatient to commence life.
I undertake to be a river to you
as you follow your course from the haven of my body to far
    distant seas.
Let yourself go, and drink up your fill.
Suck sleep from me. By the terms of the breast-contract
I'll suck back from your puckered lips
love, with which I'll suckle another time, and
for that I'm grateful.
How I welcome you, salmon of sleep
who made a tranquil pool in my life-stream.
In the rhythm of your heartbeat
I hear the music of the Heavens,
and it guides my way.

BIDDY JENKINSON (*translated from Gaelic by P. Riggs*)

from **Three Women**

FIRST VOICE:
Who is he, this blue, furious boy,
Shiny and strange, as if he had hurtled from a star?
He is looking so angrily!
He flew into the room, a shriek at his heel.
The blue color pales. He is human after all.
A red lotus opens in its bowl of blood;
They are stitching me up with silk, as if I were a material.

What did my fingers do before they held him?
What did my heart do, with its love?
I have never seen a thing so clear.
His lids are like the lilac-flower
And soft as a moth, his breath.
I shall not let go.
There is no guile or warp in him. May he keep so.

*   *   *

How long can I be a wall, keeping the wind off?
How long can I be
Gentling the sun with the shade of my hand,
Intercepting the blue bolts of a cold moon?
The voices of loneliness, the voices of sorrow
Lap at my back ineluctably.
How shall it soften them, this little lullaby?

How long can I be a wall around my green property?
How long can my hands
Be a bandage to his hurt, and my words
Bright birds in the sky, consoling, consoling?
It is a terrible thing
To be so open: it is as if my heart
Put on a face and walked into the world.

SYLVIA PLATH

Moment of Faith

It was the crying hand
Thrust from the shawl, a sharp-petalled
Celandine in cold March grass:

It was the five little swimmers,
Sea-wearied, bent at the waist,
Still waxed in each wrinkle and seam:

It was the stronghold they closed
Round her probing finger, the way
The crying shivered into stillness

That made her think that the teeming
Shambles of it all was planned,
And the plan was matchless.

CAROL RUMENS

Love & Milk

Not knowing even if you like me
    I give you milk . . . and love,
Though roughly in equal proportions,
My breasts and my heart overflowing
    for your survival.
Drawing back so as not to choke you
    with their goodness.

And giving
has become a blur
     of day and night
  and wet and dry
  and sleep and cry,
Punctuated by my warm arms
And your bright frowning eyes
    that give the lie
  to those who say you cannot yet see.
So here   in this womb of a dishevelled bed
     You   and   me,
Indulging again in
  Milk and love
    Habitually.

KRISTA DICKSON

Tender

Breasts bud the old ache of puberty,
but heavy and deeper they pull
in pains from where they join
like apples to the bough.

They will get that hard again
over a life of their own,
spurting spontaneous answers
over the arc of each hungry cry.

The cup of hands round them
cleaves energies up
from fibres that sing at the core.
Press of mouth bolts body down

with crescent lip on lip.

SUSAN TAYLOR

Daughter Dark

daughter, dark
syrup of sugarbeet,
burgundy sea;
rusty rich overture
of a black
Marram mama;
you are the bowels of Etna
opaque and flaming.
Lately I know you,
the riddle unravelling
in the scissor sun.
Your dark is all the pang
of being born.

LANNY KENNISH

Mirroring

Now he lies asleep, after the fury,
the blue of his eyelids luminous
in the cool dark;
then, one hot arm thrown across his face
as if to bar me from his dreams
dilates my eyes with tears:
this was how you slept,
this gesture so defiant
in its suffering.

You are reflections
shattering and remaking:
I remember the hot white light of birth
the searing joy as he flew,
long, slithery fish,
up out of my cut flesh,
as a soul leaves a body.
I remember the slow, brave wasting of your life
across the summer, which felt like a birth to me.

I see you in his face, my mother, as if
your breath touched him and left life there
As if I am the mirror,
and Janus-eyed I offer him to you
and offer you to him

and these shards of glass in me
are fierce birthpains
bringing love, again,
to life.

PIPPA LITTLE

To the Newborn

Like a round loaf, that's how small you were.
I rolled you on the board with my palm,
I kneaded you, patted you,
greased you smooth, floured you.
I shaped your roly body.
You slept in the palm of my hands.
You'd hardly dawned, your slight bones
were still soft under your skin, yet
how vehemently your vulnerable life
pulsed in your tiny torso, your folded limbs
closed about you like thick petals,
beneath, you slept like the still of a rose.

What kind of well is the newborn's dreams?
Where do the minute dreamers descend?
Do they summon up their seas?
Among familiar algae, again
they hide, they swim back
to timelessness' cave,
to this grotto's constant quivering dark,
the blood-red fern's nest,
down, under the blood, under destiny,

And their awakening. The breath's
laboured stirring,
until finally the will blasts
into terror's bantam blaring
To what despair
do they wake from their indifferent seas?
This wild crying, this endless
gasping, a mnemne still of their fish-life,
yet with what a voice
is their vernal despair blessed.
They sob, they clamour, they praise,
hardly alive, they meet with their throats
the assaults of reality, the million
afflictions and pleasures of matter.

And they grab what they clamoured for,
they grasp what every being grasps,
theirs the air, the earth, the milk,
the death, the lullaby, the glory.

Wrapped in a shawl you lay in your basket,
you slept, you grew plump in your dreams.
You didn't know that I took you in my arms.
I scanned your face for my lover;
the image of his face wandered across yours,
drifting like a moon in a windy sky.

What a loveliness to hold.
What a loveliness to lift.
Light as a plume, round as the sun.
My joy that drowns out everything.
The victory of intertwining limbs
against time.
He rounded in the oven of hope,
detached at the gates of expectancy.
Yet he still floats in the boundless
past, and is here too
in the still of this shawl,
in the still of this rose
he dreams his bright dream.

JUDIT TÓTH (translated from Hungarian by L. Schiff)

God

Again I can only describe it as an excess, a deep shadow
and it surrounds my darling. Or is it me?

My new child lies there
soft petal skin amidst the coral folds of his own crib

unto himself
new and smooth and clear eyed.

His shape is part of the day
as he lies there, he grows, he is fed by the sun.

But all around are the shadows
under his sweet plump body, around his crib

or are they around me?
The shadows are like a wide stretch of deep water.

I stretch out my arm –
like Adam in the creation, he reached out to God.

These waters are not mine, I will not own them
nor are they his.

So they are a deepness and darkness across which I cannot reach.
Will he reach me?

SARA BOYES

Creation

You were made
under the sea
your ear gives you away.

You were made
in the calyx of a rose
your skin betrays you.

You were made in heaven
your eyelids as you sleep
cannot disguise themselves.

You were brought to me
by a giant kite
his wings stir white

on my face still.
Never say you grew
from a seed in my body

the dandelion brought you
the spring brought you
a star with brilliant hands

delivered you
leaving his light in your eyes
as a seal, and a promise.

JENI COUZYN

In My Name

Heavy with child

belly
an arc
of black moon

I squat
over dry plantain leaves

and common the earth
to receive you

in my name
in my blood

to receive you
my curled bean
my tainted
perfect child

my bastard fruit
my seedling
my seagrape
my strange mulatto
my little bloodling

Let the snake slipping in deep grass
be dumb before you

Let the centipede writhe and shrivel
in its tracks

Let the evil one strangle on its own tongue
even as he sets his eyes upon you

For with my blood
I've cleansed you
and with my tears
I've pooled the River Niger

now my sweet one it is for you to swim

GRACE NICHOLS

The Sea at Dawn

A hopeless dawn
and the sea is high
Mother – you couldn't
comfort me – the tide
was always out. I cried
for days and nights
but not enough, the sea
alone would hold
the salt in me.

You lay there
beyond grasp

I who was born too soon,
you in your pack of ice[1]
rot in your womb.

I needed your love
then, as I do now
but you had glass arms
and your tears were frost
on my case-glass.

Your drawn face is etched
on the living-room pane
and I am not born yet.
The sea is high
your tears float there
and mix with mine

But you are locked
in a translucent zone
and it is long ago
since we were one.
They must have implanted
me in you, I suppose,
for no man
could have clasped
you in his arms
woman of snow.

I look through the window
and I am no-one
just sperm and foam.
You always wanted me
to go back
through the glass
into your vulva
your alien soul
and fling me, fling me
back to the dark

1. A treatment for septicaemia.

but you can't Mother
you were not able
the tide was always too cold, too far,
forget all your tears
I don't need you Mother –
– my darker face
in the old mirror,
I have another one
whom I call Day,
you disappear with her.

PASCALE PETIT

Premature Death

I often think of you
my boy
now thirteen

I knew you well
while you
grew in me

Seven months was
all they allowed
so they took you away

Reaching for you
but you were
already gone

Curiosity made them
cut you up
how dare they

Only to tell
that after all
you were perfect

My breasts wept
milk for you
quite useless

But you
will always remain
innocent for me

ELIZABETH BEX

My Baby Has No Name Yet

My baby has no name yet;
like a new-born chick or a puppy,
my baby is not named yet.

What numberless texts I examined
at dawn and night and evening over again!
But not one character did I find
which is as lovely as the child.
Starry field of the sky,
or heap of pearls in the depth.
Where can the name be found, how can I?

My baby has no name yet;
like an unnamed bluebird or white flowers
from the farthest land for the first,
I have no name for this baby of ours.

KIM NAM-JO (translated from Korean by Ko Won)

First Born

it was not the way I'd planned it
no rhythmic pants
between the pushes
and you wiping my brow

just a numb trickle
of being and a silence
as they sucked her out
and wrapped her in
the white sheet

left alone in the dark
I lifted her small
shocked body into my bed –
close and afraid
should I wake her

JENNIE FONTANA

Dream

Tiny, wrapped into yourself
tight as a poppy seed
precarious on my treacherous palm

and I fear to lose you
eager grass opening its teeth
earth parting her many invisible crevices

egg of a caterpillar
egg of a spider
minute human creature.

My friend seals you on a silver chain
and now little albatross
till morning comes

I wear you like a jewel.

JENI COUZYN

For a Fatherless Son

You will be aware of an absence, presently,
Growing beside you, like a tree,
A death tree, colour gone, an Australian gum tree –
Balding, gelded by lightning – an illusion,
And a sky like a pig's backside, an utter lack of attention.

But right now you are dumb.
And I love your stupidity,
The blind mirror of it. I look in
And find no face but my own, and you think that's funny.
It is good for me

To have you you grab my nose, a ladder rung.
One day you may touch what's wrong
the small skulls, the smashed blue hills,
the godawful hush.
Till then your smiles are found money.

SYLVIA PLATH

For a Child Born Dead

What ceremony can we fit
You into now? If you had come
Out of a warm and noisy room
To this, there'd be an opposite
For us to know you by. We could
Imagine you in lively mood

And then look at the other side,
The mood drawn out of you, the breath
Defeated by the power of death.
But we have never seen you stride
Ambitiously the world we know.
You could not come and yet you go.

But there is nothing now to mar
Your clear refusal of our world.
Not in our memories can we mould
You or distort your character.
Then all our consolation is
That grief can be as pure as this.

ELIZABETH JENNINGS

To Our Daughter

And she is beautiful, our daughter.
Only six months, but a person.
She turns to look at everything, out walking.
All so precious. I mustn't disturb it with words.
People are like great clowns,
Blossom like balloons, black pigeons like eagles,
Water beyond belief.

She holds out her hand to air,
Sea, sky, wind, sun, movement, stillness,
And wants to hold them all.
My finger is her earth connection, me, and earth.

Her head is like an apple, or an egg.
Skin stretched fine over a strong casing,
Her whole being developing from within
And from without: the answer.

And she sings, long notes from the belly or the throat,
Her legs kick her feet up to her nose,
She rests – laid still like a large rose.
She is our child,
The world is not hers, she has to win it.

JENIFER ARMITAGE

Poem for Jack

So finally you sleep;
the fever, the impatience
drain from the house, the rooms become cool,
I am whole, apart once more,
exhausted, a little lost.

Pale blue flush of sleep
is swelling your skin,
shadowing the eye-bone:
your hands, thrown out at each temple,
lie open, small, damp starfish.
What tears we've both cried today!
How did we manage to survive till evening!

Now I am alone, you have left me behind.
Some dream makes you smile,
a flicker of light moves through your face, is gone.
How simply you cut me out
and I am distant as a lighthouse beam
far out in the dark.

I tell myself this is the moment
I have wanted through the moiling, endless,
tangle of our day, those twisted knots
I constantly struggle to unmake

and now I am lonely, addict
of that exhaustion, unwilling
for my body to exhale your breath,
my spine to stand free of your weight.

PIPPA LITTLE

Rosie

She came from her mother
easily, without the pain
that Emma brought. She came
with a smile for the world,
'Too good to be true,'
the father said, marvelling.

She suckled intuitively,
milky as a piglet, eyes
meandering. Her mother's face
dissolved into a globe
of nourishment. Cherishing her,
they called her Rosie Jane.

'Not half the trouble
Emma was,' they said.
She slept deeply, snug
as a hot water bottle,
all night long. Her days
were placid, undemanding.

'Such a happy baby,' yet
they worried. She didn't cry.
'Not quite perfect,' doctors said.
Trusting, not comprehending tears,
Rosie laughed, a bruised plum
in the bottom of the basket.

MOIRA ANDREW

Autistic Child

Where will the wild wind blow you?
From your cage
at what age
will you let us know you?

Could I make you take my hand
look at me
lovingly
leave the ice of your land?

It is hard to read your face,
do you miss
lips to kiss
in that isolated place?

Some malfunction of the brain
keeps you safe
little waif
from the heat of our pain.

DEIRDRE ARMES SMITH

Twins

This one arrived on time
with a stitch in his side,
will reach his finishing line
a plain man, as God made him, without a single stitch on.

That one arrived clutching his brother's heel;
his emblem a ladder for he scorns the flat race.
Backed against a wall he will find
the tendril of a flowering vine and swing
upwards though his angelic challenger
awaits him smiling among the branches;
some say his mother gave him that extra push.

He protests, waving liberty's torch
that singes his spirit a little.
Outwardly he wears shirts of pure silk, flame proof and
shining smooth;
he washes and irons them himself.

GLORIA ESCOFFERY

Broken Moon
(for Emma)

Twelve, small as six,
strength, movement, hearing
all given in half measure,
my daughter,
child of genetic carelessness,
walks uphill, always.

I watch her morning face;
precocious patience as she hooks each sock,
creeps it up her foot,
aims her jersey like a quoit.
My fingers twitch;
her private frown deters.

Her jokes can sting:
'My life is like dressed crab
– lot of effort, rather little meat.'
Yet she delights in seedlings taking root,
finding a fossil,
a surprise dessert.

Chopin will not yield to her stiff touch;
I hear her cursing.
She paces Bach exactly,
firm rounding of perfect cadences.
Somewhere inside
she is dancing a courante.

In dreams she skims the sand,
curls toes into the ooze of pools,
leaps on to stanchions.
Awake, her cousins take her hands;
they lean into the waves,
stick-child between curved sturdiness.

She turns away from stares,
laughs at the boy who asks
if she will find a midget husband.
Ten years ago, cradling her,
I showed her the slice of silver in the sky.
'Moon broken,' she said.

CAROLE SATYAMURTI

No sadness in her play only in your look
(1982)

warm amazing small body
on my skin dashed with blood

and to see that one arm ended short
with no hand

someone said it's a girl
and I said she's only got one hand
and there was silence in the room

a soft rounded arm
that meant
you have no hand on that side

after the shock of that labour
this baby not yet real

we've never seen this before
    never seen a baby come out
    grey motionless   Hanging over
    the midwife's hands
    curved grey body drooping

and then they talked of heart defects
and you snuffled
and I wondered   why this   why us
but you lived   and lived

I was constantly amazed by your livingness
and taken up with myself
the pain of my labour   my adjustment to a baby

A transition   gradual
yes   painful to take you in public
they will look
they do stare   for a moment   and
speak to their companion
– oh dear
what a shame poor little thing –
 but more difficult just learning   to be
 with a baby

Tiny baby   how unreal and real you are
powerfully creating every moment of work for me
 to turn the world inside out again
 for both of us
every moment of self recognition
forcing me to look up   look behind
glance everywhere   grasp and tangle
with the inside the cords
veins   nerves   threads

She is not a   what a shame   she is
playing   absorbed in her doingness

no sadness in her play   only in your look
which will slowly   but I hope never

sink into her wholeness
myself   herself   complete

CAROLINE HALLIDAY

My daughter and I are proud of our part in raising awareness around disability
issues. It is the responsibility of all of us to change our attitudes, from
'separateness', to celebration of difference and disability.

Babel

What angel has taken up residence in your mouth?
What half-made spirit sits on your lips, babbling child,
proclaiming your latest, equivocal gift? You rhyme
with whistling birds or engines that groan or yammer;
the voices of the world which prick your small
impartial ear you scatter back in serious jest. Syllables
of untrimmed meaning string a broken sentence
on a single breath – hooting demonstratives, precision
trills, triumphing shrieks, an old man's mimicked
cough. Speaking without falseness, you talk
in tongues: your new occupation is our Babel-past.
There was, in the story, a vast and sunswept
plain where a windy tower held sky
to ground. Its builders yelled across the flinging
spaces, mocking each other's prattle, spitting
and summoning the gods to inspect their work.
They remember when their voices were inhuman,
guiltless and had no echo. Now we are the jealous
deities of speech, exacting for our one gift
the muteness which keeps you whole, unmemoried.
We watch our work: language condenses quickly
out of its natal mist into shapes that can turn
cartwheels, eat fire and inflame the earth;
make wars, break promises, stamp gold.
The daimon utters, the sorcery has begun.
But no words will be as literal as your lovely
jargon, words do not speak in tongues, which
soon you will outgrow and then forget. Against
that sadness, this proprietorial wish – still may
your human voice be single, a neighbourhood of spirits.

LESLEY SAUNDERS

Death of a Young Son by Drowning

He, who navigated with success
the dangerous river of his own birth
once more set forth

on a voyage of discovery
into the land I floated on
but could not touch to claim.

His feet slid on the bank,
the currents took him;
he swirled with ice and trees in the swollen water

and plunged into distant regions,
his head a bathysphere;
through his eyes' thin glass bubbles

he looked out, reckless adventurer
on a landscape stranger than Uranus
we have all been to and some remember.

There was an accident; the air locked,
he was hung in the river like a heart.
They retrieved the swamped body,

cairn of my plans and future charts,
with poles and hooks
from among the nudging logs.

It was spring, the sun kept shining, the new grass
leapt to solidity;
my hands glistened with details.

After the long trip I was tired of waves.
My foot hit rock. The dreamed sails
collapsed, ragged.

>   I planted him in this country
>   like a flag.

MARGARET ATWOOD

Yet Another Poem about a Dying Child

Poet and parents say he cannot die
so young, so tied to trees and stars.
Their word across his mouth obscures
and cures his murmuring goodbye.
He babbles (they say), of spring flowers,

Who for six months has lain
his flesh at a touch bruised violet,
his face pale, his hate clearer
than milky love that would smooth over
the pebbles of diseased bone.

Pain spangles him like the sun.
He cries and cannot say why.
His blood blossoms like a pear tree.
He does not want to eat or keep
its ugly windfall fruit.

He does not want to spend or share
the engraved penny of light
that birth put in his hand
telling him to hold it tight.
Will parents and poets not understand?

He must sleep, rocking the web of pain
till the kind funnel spider will come
with the night-lamp eyes and soft tread
to wrap him warm and carry him home
to a dark place, and eat him.

JANET FRAME

Rocks & Stones & Trees

I dreamt I went looking for you, down a flight
of stone steps, past a chapel, or a palace:
you held my hand, but I never saw your face,
and when we reached the foot of the tall steps

you vanished. Your blood-cells would not multiply
as they were meant to. Drifting out of our air,
six-year-old flesh and ghost, beyond the rim
of the whirling earth, no one can find you now.

When my son was newly born, I used to dream,
night, that I lost him, or I left him
alone in the darkened house, or overlay him,
or found him stolen. But later I forgot.

Lucy, we are all in the dark: we love
where we have no right; we steal what belongs to others,
and leave what is ours abandoned to the air
at the top of the steps. We are all lost, as you are.

MARGARET CRANE

Child of Our Time

Yesterday. I knew no lullaby
But you have taught me overnight to order
This song, which takes for your final cry
Its tune, from your unreasoned end its reason;
Its rhythm from the discord of your murder
Its motive from the fact you cannot listen.

We who should have known how to instruct
with rhymes for your waking, rhythms for your sleep,
Names for the animals you took to bed,
Tales to distract, legends to protect,
Later an idiom for you to keep
and living, learn, must learn for you dead.

To make our broken images rebuild
Themselves around your limbs, your broken
Image, find for your sake whose life our idle
talk has cost, a new language. Child
of our time, our times have robbed your cradle.
Sleep in a world your final sleep has woken.

EAVAN BOLAND

from A Matter of Life and Death

Down the porphyry stair
Headlong into the air
The boy has come: he crouches there
A tender startled creature
With a fawn's ears and hair-spring poise
Alert to every danger
Aghast at every noise.
A blue blink
From under squeezed-up lids
As mauve as iris buds
Is gone as quickly as a bird's bright wink.
Gone – but as if his soul had looked an instant through the
    chink.
And perfect as his shell-like nails,
Close as are to the flower its petals,
My love unfolded with him.
Yet till this moment what was he to me?
Conjecture and analogy;
Conceived and yet unknown;
Behind this narrow barrier of bone
Distant as any foreign land could be.

* * *

His smiles are all largesse
Need ask for no return,
Since give and take are meaningless
To one who gives by needing

And takes our love for granted
And grants a favour even by his greed.
The ballet of his twirling hands
His chirping and his loving sounds,
Perpetual expectation
Perpetual surprise –
Not a lifetime satisfies
For watching, every thing he does
We wish him to do always.

> *Only in a lover's eyes*
> *Shall I be so approved again;*
> *Only the other side of pain*
> *Can truth again be all I speak,*
> *Or I again possess*
> *A saint's hilarious carelessness.*

ANNE RIDLER

MOTHERHOOD

Can't Not Never Do Nothing Right

Mother Funk

I'm a post-depressionist, self-expressionist,
True confessionist woman.
I've got more than one string to my ham.
I am the degeneration gap,
Pre-shrunk, past punk
Seminal derivitor of
Mother Funk.

I'm a Spock 'n Roll, stockin' roll Mama,
I've got low expectations of all relations
That make High Drama.
Got the valium-yums, got the shrinks and the kinks.
All that flab and the mini pants,
Menopause renaissance junk.
I got Mother Funk.

I was the pre-pill pillar of the whole megillah,
Read novels, dieted, while hot beds rioted.
What did I get? Nyet.
Angst for the mammeries,
Consultant Samurai's took a chunk.
Then I heard reveille, got myself heavily
Into Mother Funk.

Want to bust the cage, find the Fountain of Middle Age,
Spread ugly roomers, transplant sense of humours,
Grow a moustache, flash!
Draw my perimeters, immature similars
Need not apply until I
Grab my hunk
Of Mother Funk.

I'm an existentialist with a shopping list,
Post partumultuous creature.
A double breasted double feature,
One woman rhythm band . . . parenthood wasn't planned,
Jives to the pipes of a different plumber,
Sings till I'm sunk
In Mother Funk.

I may flunk the means test, the old baggy jeans test
Won't darken my Dior. The poor are so pure.
I'm slumming down market and love it. I'll lark it
This missions position is: Ma's on top.
Mama cop rules in this bunk . . .
It's all Mother Funk.

I'm a fully gendered, single entendred
Open ended Ms.
Haven't forgotten what I've begotten, which is
Daughters, reporters of current affairs.
Their poor old dad thinks the harem's gone mad,
And while he says his prayers,
I'm power drunk
On Mother Funk.

JOAN VAN POZNAK

This Belonging, This Us
(for Ian, Phoebe and Beatrice)

Our tiny childrens' hearts are lanterns
Of promise   we are led
and in turn lead by the moss stones   the coral
bark of stripped chestnut wood.
Forgive my hands
                their shakedness. The river's
dark silt tenders less. Take hold this steady heart.
Forgive my tears
                their wetness. The crumpled
paper's damp hand. Remind me of the short seasons
that can cut off a young life.
Forgive my greed
                its youthfulness. The dark trees
at night are only the dark trees of the daytime.
Give up worry and torture.

Life is OK.
It has a lot to recommend it.
By and large.

He lifted up his head.
He lifted up his head all branched made.

Women snap
break the tender days
trapped between their bowed bodies
                 guilty hearts.
Children's small fears, open faces
trusted and held. Taunt the women's thirst of love.

Gladly gladly suckle.

ELAINE RANDELL

Family

There are times
when out of the wearing
tearing of noise and task
the exhaustion of distraction
the muddling daily round
of burden of bond

We come together
roll into one body
man, woman, child
and are fallen
entirely in love
belonging together

we laugh raucously
and delight in our
secret affinity
all touching, smiling
and belly-goodness
feasting and treats.

Strange this
preference for blood
Is it self-protection
or narrow narcissism?
But yet how healing is
this duty of nourishment.

My poverty falls away
my flesh fills out
I am woven into this
strong meshing of lives
we spread out, are extended
a little of each in the other.

There are times
when all rolled up
blended into one
we swim through the air
a brilliant fish
into the liquid eye of life.

ROSEMARY PALMEIRA

Cobweb

They are caught in this enchanted house
by frost and a little snow at the door.
He sleeps again in a narrow bed.
She listens to a small breathing in the corner;
the new travel cot of striped net
is placed on a floor of blackened timber.

The room below is lit.
Light races through pin-hole cracks in the wood.
Her sleeping baby is weaver;
he pulls her like weft through a warp of love.
She dances on a dark oak sky
through a mesh of man-made stars.

SUSAN TAYLOR

The Mother in the Afternoons

The summer woman goes loose down,
goes floosing down
with the dog trailing
past the leaves frilling
to the school's shadows
in the mid-afternoon.

And the woman comes back autumn.
Harvested.
Her three children spinning
and shuffling and scattering.

And with her blue cotton billows
she wraps up,
brings the children in,
bringing the children in.

KAY SYRAD

Fantasy Mother

the love of my life
my heroine   my sweetheart   my goddess
protects consoles and loves loves loves
me
and exists in my head
alongside
        nightmares   hallucinations   delirium

She never never turns away from me
She never never goes away from me
She never never speaks to me except
with pearls and rubies in her voice
and in her nightly lullabies.

She smells of
wisteria and honeysuckle and lily of the valley
her hair is thick and waved on her head
like petals

her hands are cool   tapered   gentle
her feet are long   fine   cool

her face offers
acceptance
of all i am

ASTRA

Everybody's Mother

Of course
everybody's mother always and
so on . . .

Always never
loved you enough
or too smothering much.

Of course you were the Only One, your
mother
a machine
that shat out siblings, listen

everybody's mother
was the original Frigid-
aire Icequeen clunking out
the hardstuff in nuggets, mirror
silvers and ice-splinters that'd stick
in your heart.

Absolutely everyone's mother
was artistic when she was young.

Everyone's mother
was a perfumed presence with pearls, remote
white shoulders when she
bent over in her ball dress
to kiss you in your crib.

Everybody's mother slept with the butcher
for sausages to stuff you with.

Everyone's mother
mythologised herself. You got mixed up
between dragon's teeth and blackmarket stockings.

Naturally
she failed to give you
Positive Feelings
about your own sorry
sprouting body (it was a bloody shame)

but she did
sit up all night sewing sequins
on your carnival costume

so you would have a good time

and she spat
on the corner of her hanky and scraped
at your mouth with sour lace till you squirmed
so you would look smart

And where
was your father all this time?
Away
at the war, or
in his office, or any-
way conspicuous for his
Absence, so

what if your mother did
float around above you
big as a barrage balloon
blocking out the light?

Nobody's mother can't not never do nothing right.

LIZ LOCHHEAD

Song for a Young Mother

There, there, you fit my lap
Like an acorn to its cup,
Your weight upon my arm
Is like a golden plum,
Like an apple in the hand
Or a stone on the ground.

As a bird in the fallow
scoops a shallow hollow
Where the earth's upward pressing
Answers egg and nestling
– Earth's mass and beginning
Of all their learning –

So you learn from my arm
You have substance and a house
So I learn from your birth
that I am not vague and wild
But as solid as my child
And as constant as the earth.

EDITH SCOVELL

The Scream

I fan love on to this hot child
because I cannot bear the screaming
that topples my head.

I know a tired baby must scream,
but I wedge concern like cotton wool
into each little despair.

The screamings take us back
to that blasted birth;
its crucial agony of breath.

I farm love out as comfort
over many acres of panic,
yet still it grows.

SUSAN TAYLOR

To My Sister

You have laid your heart out
flat as a rug,
wrapped children in it.
You have gathered them like flowers from mist,
out of time

plucked them firm as apples.
Mine was a windfall fruit
and you watched her shrivel
before turning
with hands outstretched for more.

Courage, I call it,
this turning a still face
to the gyring helix;
making blood of shadows past
flesh of the unseen.

You were the quiet one
who hid from danger
tucked yourself away on plains
in small towns;
who did not climb too high.

Where is she now
that girl who whimpered at shadows?
She is singing in the dark
rocking and rocking
fear out.

JENNY VUGLAR

Natural High

my mother is a
red
woman

she
gets high
on clean children

grows
common sense

injects
tales
with heroines

fumes
over dirty habits

hits the sky
on bad lines

cracking meteors

my mother
gets red
with the sun

JEAN BINTA BREEZE

Her Belly

She has a right to have a fat belly,
her belly has borne five children.
They warmed themselves at it,
it was the sun of their childhood.

The five children have gone,
her fat belly remains.
This belly
is beautiful.

ANNA SWIR

Breathing

Each day the water gathers.
Sometimes just enough
to soften the hard edges of the doorways
to dissolve
the necessity of cleaning, dusting
the more extreme reaches
of painting of furniture, making new curtains.

But sometimes so much
because I am given over to the baby, that my needs
float, half submerged
on the waters of barely noted feeling.
Then the water rises
logging the spare needs of each day. Eating a meal
or shopping, or washing up.

Now I lower myself into the salt water.
               I am the novice swimmer
who must swim or will drown.
Or shall I just float here, a while
               in amongst the sodden wreckage.
The armchair, misshapen with water. The carpet
the dead jungle muddied with run colours.

               Only this smallest breath
as I lift my head for air and my lungs
with difficulty pump out the water.
               Only this smallest breath of air
which insists in its own movement, in and out –
more, I will have more. I breathe
I will breathe more.

SARA BOYES

Middle-Aged Motherhood

They want me all the time
not me
of course
nor anything I have
or have to offer.
But whatever it is
they want it all the time
and always from me.

SUSANNAH LASH

The Woman with Too Many Children Already

Is truly in a shoe
tied up tied down expecting
another she grabs the toddler

by the shirt back
balancing baby on her square hip
slicing with one hand the evening
supper again
again attention sprawls
in every direction she calls to stop
that Daddy's gonna hear about
their mouths the constant
question what
to put into them.
Answers, tries
to fill demands
but needs an hour a long
vacation.
She's not that basket
of bread replenished
not even recharged at the dinner hour
but eats in jerks and angry
can't
though when she sees those
fighting brothers
collapsed in bed their arms
around each other
sleeping links them
all she feels
it must be worth it.

LAURA CHESTER

Mother's Catalogue

I hate you for not leaving me be,
for crying even harder when I hit you,
I hate you for making me shake you,
for clinging to me and needing me
when I don't want anything more to do with you.
I hate you for not doing what I want you to do,
for not going to sleep so I can have some time,

for not letting me sleep, I hate you for stopping me
doing all the things I would do if you weren't here.
I hate you for having a life of your own.

And I hate you for making me a mother
– in other words, housewife –
and we don't even believe in marriage!
I hate you for refusing to see when I break
into a million pieces and silently scream myself
to death, invisible blood running down the kichen walls.
I hate you for not doing things my way
and for just not doing things,
I hate you for being other than me.

I hate you for being better mothers than me,
for not being mothers in the first place,
for spending more time with your children than I do,
putting them first, I hate you for putting yourselves first,
I hate you for having the energy to do more
or for being content to do less,
for teaching, for writing, for learning to dance,
for going on holiday in the winter, for working things out
    better.
I hate you for having nicer births, babies, places to live,
I hate you for making me compare myself with you.

Sometimes I am so consumed with hate
I turn the world to stone when I look in the glass.
I am the madwoman, the witch.

Sometimes I need my hate to help me stay alive.

LESLEY SAUNDERS

Christmas Carols

Children do not always mean
hope. To some they mean despair.
This woman with her hair cut off
so she could not hang herself
threw herself from a rooftop, thirty
times raped and pregnant by the enemy
who did this to her. This one had her pelvis
broken by hammers so the child
could be extracted. Then she was thrown away,
useless, a ripped sack. This one
punctured herself with kitchen skewers
and bled to death on a greasy
oilcloth table, rather than bear
again and past limit. There is a limit, though who knows
when it may come? Nineteenth century
ditches are littered with small wax corpses
dropped there in terror. A plane
swoops too low over the fox farm
and the mother eats her young. This too
is Nature. Think twice then
before you worship turned furrows, or pay
the magic mother, in blue
and white, upon that pedestal,
perfect and intact, distinct
from those who aren't. Which means
everyone else. It's a matter
of food and available blood. If mother-
hood is sacred, put
your money where your mouth is. Only
then can you expect the coming
down to the wretched and shimmering earth
of that miracle you sing
about, the day
when every child is a holy birth.

MARGARET ATWOOD

Unknown Girl in the Maternity Ward

Child, the current of your breath is six days long.
You lie, a small knuckle on my white bed;
lie, fisted like a snail, so small and strong
at my breast. Your lips are animals; you are fed
with love. At first hunger is not wrong.
The nurses nod their caps; you are shepherded
down starch halls with the other unnested throng
in wheeling baskets. You tip like a cup; your head
moving to my touch. You sense the way we belong.

But this is an institution bed.
You will not know me very long.

The doctors are enamel. They want to know
the facts. They guess about the man who left me,
some pendulum soul, going the way men go
and leave you full of child. But our case history
stays blank. All I did was let you grow.
Now we are here for all the ward to see.
They thought I was strange, although
I never spoke a word. I burst empty
of you, letting you learn how the air is so.
The doctors chart the riddle they ask of me
and I turn my head away. I do not know.

Yours is the only face I recognise.
Bone at my bone, you drink my answers in.
Six times a day I prize
your need, the animals of your lips, your skin
growing warm and plump. I see your eyes
lifting their tents. They are blue stones, they begin
to outgrow their moss. You blink in surprise
and I wonder what you can see, my funny kin,
as you trouble my silence. I am a shelter of lies.
Should I learn to speak again, or hopeless in
such sanity will I touch some face I recognise?

Down the hall the baskets start back. My arms
fit you like a sleeve, they hold
catkins of your willows, the wild bee farms
of your nerves, each muscle and fold
of your first days. Your old man's face disarms
the nurses. But the doctors return to scold
me. I speak. It is you my silence harms.
I should have known; I should have told
them something to write down. My voice alarms
my throat. 'Name of father – none.' I hold
you and name you bastard in my arms.
And now that's that. There is nothing more
that I can say or lose.

Others have traded life before
and could not speak. I tighten to refuse
your owling eyes, my fragile visitor.
I touch your cheeks, like flowers. You bruise
against me. We unlearn. I am a shore
rocking you off. You break from me. I choose
your only way, my small inheritor
and hand you off, trembling the selves we lose.
Go child, who is my sin and nothing more.

ANNE SEXTON

Signing Him Away

For eighteen years I waited for his call,
And when it came
I feared his voice. I heard the same brutal
Seduction, the same
Dark timbre. Double pain.

And I'd be lacking all the qualities
Surrounding him:
No clever turn of phrase, no sparkling speech
To wallpaper my shame,
No childhood clichés.

No day without a thought for him, always
Regret at signing
Him away. Oh, but his eyes
Would burn and sting,
Would sue my dreams,

Would claim his other life, and mine.
I sit here trembling
Waiting for his face, not knowing
How to mime the mother role, dreading
His footfall and the ring

I cannot answer.

LOTTE KRAMER

The Woman with a Love Child

As we locked bodies and gripped for the gateway
I knew
someone burst into being
an angel out of nothing
and I carried him high
through those nine month miles, despite their questions
and I sang to the wet winds
that took away the father he would never know
but it didn't seem to matter.
He swam out of my womb a love child
smooth as a swan
black as a swan
and when he smiled for the first time, my heart
beat its heavy wings
until the air stirred around us.
And when the government voice
said bastard, state, belongings –
we flew, we flew.

LAURA CHESTER

The Lost Child

She walks with me in my sleep, her hand
given to mine the distance of a long dream
or a trust too ordinary to mention.

Her hair is light with the sun, but brown
as a secret at the bobbed line. She is perhaps
eight –

         or she appears
knee-deep in waves at noon, solemn behind
snorkel and mask, intent,

forgetting I'm there. She is always some-
one else's child or no-one's.
                The worst I think

is when she is half asleep on my lap,
arms holding, her body warm
and certain against mine, comforted
                     comforting.

RUTH VALENTINE

from Placenta Praevia

& all those years nobody loved me
except her & I screamed at her & spanked
her
& threw her on the bed & slammed the
door when
i was angry & desperate for her
father's love,
& I cant undo all those times i frightened her
& she loved me, she still loves me,
i cant undo needing &
being tortured with loneliness

until I cried out at her,
who loved me even in my needy loneliness. & how
do mothers, unloved, love their children?
the wonder is that we do, we
do not leave the little girl, we
do not destroy
we cry out in terror we love
our little girls
who must have a better life . . .

ALTA

Heavy as Lead

I   For our children are the children of our flesh
And the body of our love . . . love that was
Before childbirth seems airy, feathery,
Frond-like now, a spirit moving grass.

Lovers' love which is a spirit must take
Flesh, the bodies we beget and bear;
And flesh is heavy and opaque
And a lodestone to care.

II Heavy as lead, heavy as water
That sinks with obdurate art
and finds for resting-place the deepest part,
So heavy in us is our tender daughter.

Heavy in us – to God or stranger
A spirit or leaf-light sapling,
To us she is a leaden anchor grappling
To sand and central rock; the ocean deep or

Strains against it. Heavy as earth
On a trees' roots when the green tree
Its sunward frame, is racing like a sea.

So heavy is child-love, and holds us as if she,
O child, were ground that gave us birth.

EDITH SCOVELL

The Vigil

(Rizpah protects her executed sons from carrion and beast,
Samuel 2.21)

I The grain of my skin
is this sack-cloth
spread on rock

my senses
nest in the crags
strain with winged and footed
approaches

Footholds slip helplessly
from me

mistaking the wailing
cries of the jackal for my own
grief. — The

wolves for the
raging beast at my breast-cage

The sky gashes open

They are falling still

II As long as I could
cradle their heads
stroke their hair off their
temples, the way I did when they were
children, and
hid in my skirt

I kept up my strength with
pomegranates; the sparse figs

(barley scythes
thresh in my head – not one
grain passes my lips)

I wet a cloth
in the scant stream
bathed them and Merab's sons
rubbed them in oil of spikenard

but I could not keep them clean

the stench spasms my belly
– labouring these limbs –
hardly able to tell Mephibosheth
from Armoni   expelled from me.

III   but in this torn sky, these stars that
suck the water-hole

   • I recall Armoni's eyes
soft as a gazelle's

Mephibosheth
nimble as a roebuck
could hear the grass
curve beneath a lizard
the sand swerve beneath
a scorpion

I ward off the
flesh-grazing shadows
the vultures that
thicken and darken

kneel on the floor
of the mountain
as if I could overwhelm
its stone with ledges

ease my sons
out of this death

through the lilies of the field
the darnel grasses

back to my womb
                – parched
split cedar boughs
drinking the rain

growing whole

LINDA ROSE PARKES

This Yonder Night I Sawe a Sighte

This yonder night I sawe a sighte:
A sterre as bright as ony daye;
And ever amonge a maidene songe,
'By by, lully, lullaye.'

This maiden hight Mary, she was full milde,
She knelede bifore here owne dere childe.
    She lullede, she lappede,
    She rullede, she wrapped,
    She wepped withoutene nay;
    She rullede him, she dressede him,
    She sange: 'Dere sone, lullay.'

She saide: 'Dere sone, ly still and slepe,
What cause hast thu so sore to wepe.
    With sighing and sobbinge;
    With crying and with scrycchinge,
    All this londe-day;
    And thus wakinge with sore wepinge,
    With many salt teres droppinge?
    Ly stille, dere sone, I thee pray.'

'Moder,' he saide, 'for man I wepe so sore
And for his love I shall be tore
   With scourging, with thretning,
   With bobbing, with beting –
   For sothe, moder, I saye –
   And on a crosse full by hanging,
   And to my herte foll sore sticking
   A spere on Good Fridaye.'

This maidene aunswerede with hevy chere:
'Shalt thu thus sofere, my swete sone dere?
   Now I morne, now I muse,
   I all gladness refuse –
   I, ever for this day.
   My dere sone, I thee pray,
   This paine thu put away,
   And if it possibil be may.'

ANON *(Medieval lyric)*

Madonna and Child[1]

I are one in a womb of stone –
   bianca del mare – whiteness of water
   and stone in which love is.

Faces and hands hold, touch
in total tenderness.
Sheltering arms

offer brief safety.
Her eyes and delicate mouth
prepare for grief.

1. The Madonna and Child sculpture in St Ives' church was carved in memory of Barbara Hepworth's eldest son Paul, killed in an accident while flying for the RAF in Thailand in 1953.

II I do not know their dolour –
mothers who live on
when their grown child is dead.

But when a baby died,
fell lifeless from me
before he saw the world

beautiful and cruel,
my grieving arms
felt emptied of flesh.

ANNE BORN

Planting Children, 1939

Oh quick, garner the children
stash them in baskets, egg crates,
dresser drawers, anywhere;
kiss their thin necks in the hollow
where the blood pulses,
kiss their warm ears. The train already
is raising dust,
the lists are drawn up, the cows
no longer look up from pasture.
It is the iron hinge the parting.
Now, quick, shove the babies underground
like spuds: let them root there
for forty years, let them
come up storytellers, all eyes.

EVAN ZIMROTH

The Black and Tans Deliver Her Cousin's Son
(Galway 1921)

'Didn't she step out into the yard
God love her
and see her own son's brains
scattered like mash about the flags?
And didn't she kneel down
and gather the soggy shards
of her womb's child into her apron
carefully, as a girl gathers
mushrooms in the September fields?
And didn't she then stifle
the outbreath of her grieving
till only a whistle
or whimper of her lamentation
was heard in that place lest
the soldiers note her the more?'

CATHERINE BYRON

Woman of El Salvador

My strong sons,
sweeter than star apples,
both murdered,
all gone.

My firstborn,
I was just a girl,
his father vigorous, *guapo*
(we heard humming birds
where we lay
and afterwards ate mango),
a proud man,
straight coco palm,
like our son Humberto
when they gunned him down.

My strong sons,
sweeter than *chiche coyol*.[1]
both murdered,
all gone.

And my little one,
my Coquito,
my clever monkey.
I nursed him long,
my last time,
till he was bored and naughty,
tweaking and nipping
so I let him go.
He was always impatient
to be a man,
foolhardy, accident prone.
But he was just thirteen,
a boy still, wiry liana,
when they gunned him down.

My strong sons,
sweeter than wild bee honey,
both murdered,
all gone.

> Must everything we cherish,
> nurture and watch grow
> fall to the destroyer?
> Why does their heavy hand
> smash all we have done,
> kill and kill and kill?
> They are cruel past all reason.
> It is beyond understanding.

I was a ripe calabash.
I shrivel like last year's almond.
I am an empty gourd.
I am stripped maize

---

1. *Chiche coyol* is a drink made of palm juice.

but my harvest is wasted.
My arms hang slack.

I have seen their wanton destruction
go on and on and on,
my people's pain my own,
many mothers weeping for their children,
dead bodies piled like rubbish,
many sons and daughters
mothers fathers friends
all murdered,
all gone.
Let it end.

DINAH LIVINGSTONE

Woman in a Tableau
(after an incident in the Sahel region reported by a UNICEF *official)*

dust colours her face

                    nightmare

drought

                    water polluted

the choice between

                    giving her child watery mud

and letting him die

                    seeing the choice

over and over

                    telling her hands

becoming the choice

                    giving the baby poisoned water

his tongue burning now

                    forever against hers

KATHERINE GALLAGHER

Reflection
'I Love My Children More Than Anyone'

How I wish I could discern
why
children once arriving
overturn our world,
disqualifying ourselves
to them, – reproachless
and how we turn our
necks inward
on their depth,
like swans relishing
to capture lives underneath.

But I understand
though the need
of lover and friend
that they do not possess
the gleam
which gilds the lake
with innocence;
when we protect
the small ones from the snatching world
of coarse grass:

for in them
are our tomorrows,
unnerving dives,
floaters of calm.

And in their gaze
absence of arrogance,
which is more than
a bait for our being.

MENNA ELFYN *(translated from the Welsh by the author)*

Children

Whether by careless accident
or careful plan
we are where they begin.

They grow in us
like germs or fictions
and we grow big with them.

Red, mewling strangers
they tear our thresholds
and immediately we love them.

When people say
they look like us
we smile and blush.

We listen for their cries
as if we felt their pain
and hunger deep in us

and hold them tightly
in our arms as if we'd found
a lost part of ourselves.

We want to give them
all the things we never had,
to make it up to them

for all the times
when we were hurt or sad,
to start again and put right

our mistakes in them,
to run in front of them
with warning flags.

We who've failed to be
the authors of our lives
write theirs.

We make them heroes,
stars whose happy endings
will scatter light in ours.

We feed them with our dreams
then wait and watch
like gardeners for flowers.

VICKI FEAVER

A Long Way from Georgia
(for Eva, 1900–1988)

Earth-mothers come from that earth-mother land,
where meat-filled cabbage and good bread blend
with eastern spice and southern sun.

Their cuisine is a rich substantial mix
of ancient recipes, acted out.
Tiny women: their robust arms
stretch around vast vats of food
in unending preparation for those they love.
Vibrant laughter, rooted in earth,
garnishes menus simmered in emotions.

Such a one was this mother.

Like a turtle she crawled over scorching sand
to care for her brood, scooping out protection;
swimming between cultures, continents,
absorbing new tongues with each transition.
She ploughed through seas of 'shifté-shaah',[1]
scaling mountains of rice and 'gigar';[2]
cooking futures with unfailing precision,
dispensing meatballs, rich with compassion.

---

1. Thick yellow-pea soup
2. Liver, also used as a term of endearment

All this we'll remember: truth and humour,
wafting from kitchens spiced with hillsides,
– coriander for comfort, the directness of dill;
generous servings, heaped and steaming
with the fragrance and passion of Eva's life.

CAROLYN ASKAR

A Cycle of Women

It is that dream world Anaïs speaks of
that dark watery place
where everything is female
where you open the door of the house
and she waits upstairs
the way you knew she would
and her hair floats over the world.

Every woman has a history
mother and grandmother and the ones before that
the faces she sees in dreams or visions
and wonders *Who?* A childless woman
waking at night to the hard pull, the old
contractions, the birth cry of her mothers.
Or the heaviness in her back from stooping,
her hips from iron belts, the lines in
her face from mountain women.

Or longer ago than that, the spears
and battleaxes, that ache in the thighs
from straining tight on the horses.
And the old queens, before history began,
when it was her story they told,
did they wrap their heads in bright cloth,
wear bracelets? Or were they nude
and savage, their breasts large and
firm, their feet solid on their solid earth?

Each one is queen, mother, huntress
though each remembers little of it
and some remember nothing at all,
resting in crazy houses
from the long spin of history
drinking the grief of their sex
eating it in bitter pills
muttering in kitchens,
telling their daughters
the story of the sleeping princess
but knowing it takes more than a man's kiss
to wake one so bent on sleeping her life away.

Someone who should be kept in an ice-box
until she is ready; then wake her up, as now,
into a cave or a field,
using perhaps the kiss of a sister.
Let her go from there, start over,
live it again, until she knows who she is.
Until she rises as though from the sea
not on the half-shell this time
nothing to laugh at
and not as delicate as he imagined her:
a woman big-hipped, beautiful, and fierce.

SHARON BARBA

LETTING GO

Where The Mesh Is Wound

Song of the Almost Remembered

Your trust betrayed me. Child
I am not your mother, nor ever
could be. Never trust me.

don't come near me with your
dear crying. I am the one
who dies when you need me

I am the one who is not there
the absent one, that particular
ache inside you, half knowledge

of something lost that was never
quite answered. No I am not
your mother, not your child

never your beloved. I am the one
who passes across your dreams
the almost remembered.

Little smiling thing, arms
lifted like beating wings
I am the far off

light on the hills
in your private night where you are
vomiting with fear.

They will come back
with their strangeness and their healing
and take you away and I will be

utterly gone from you
again and again and again. There is no
protection in me although

little occupant
I am rigid with losing you
everywhere we go.

JENI COUZYN

Breathing

I used to hover
at the ribs of my daughter's crib
resting my hand
on the rise/fall of her chest,
quickening like a bird's.

Later I started
listening to my husband,
to each time he lost – and caught –
his breath.
I became the landlord of breathing

and know its grammar:
its assertions and longing, its
crocus-shape, its radical
hesitations.
Now there are two daughters,
the same husband, all
breathing, all somehow
making it 'til morning.

Still I attend these quilted
nightly monologues:
I cannot yet
breathe easy.

EVAN ZIMROTH

Lullaby

Go to sleep, Mum,
I won't stop breathing
suddenly, in the night.

Go to sleep, I won't
climb out of my cot and
tumble downstairs.

Mum, I won't swallow
the pills the doctor gave you or
put hairpins in electric
sockets, just go to sleep.

I won't cry
when you take me to school and leave me:
I'll be happy with other children
my own age.

Sleep, Mum, sleep.
I won't
fall in the pond, play with matches,
run under a lorry or even consider
sweets from strangers.

No, I won't
give you a lot of lip,
not like some.

I won't sniff glue
fail all my exams
get myself/
my girlfriend pregnant.
I'll work hard and get a steady/
really worthwhile job.
I promise, go to sleep.

I'll never forget
to drop in/phone/write
and if
I need any milk, I'll yell.

ROSEMARY NORMAN

Filling the Spaces

Love and need conceived them
to fill the blank space,
that moment in the bloody darkness.

Huge helmets of bone
lay snug and tiny petalled mouths
sucked sprouting fingers,
budding clusters of pink anemones.

Nine months of bliss we had,
you anchored like a boat to my belly,
rocking, rocking
in silvered amniotic oceans.

Still I hold
the memory of the moment
we first met,
separate, human
face to face,
I cried at your completeness
and the pain
of knowing this was
already the beginning of the end.

You have grown:
seedlings nurtured
by my need, reaching out
towards
the light,
the moment
of your own flowering.

And I am thrown back
as you rush careless from the house,
heads stuffed with football and friends,
to that blank space,
seeking new labels and definitions
among the dirty socks
and discarded breakfast things.

SUE HUBBARD

Lost

Our child lost in Kew Gardens –
acres, acres and us peeling back
the unimaginable,
desperate for another chance . . . .

Tourists passed smiling – blossoms, trees
blurred into policemen's radios,
children's cries cutting –
a three-year-old's blind signals.

He had gone, vanished
while we raced the afternoon's
frenetic maze, dread and nausea
jagging our ribs.

An hour's nightmares magnified –
waiting in one place as directed,
with reassurances gathering like balloons,
plummeting to a despair.

Suddenly my mother, stern heart
moored between separations, deaths
and years of loving, stood there
marking time, waiting too.

KATHERINE GALLAGHER

The Children Are Late

The children are late.
They are buried on the motorway in a tangle of wreckage.
Soon she will hear it on the news.
Didn't she always know this would happen?
Their photographs, beside the clock, display the cleft between
  her hope and fear.

Where the Mesh is Wound

The girl's back is snapped, limbs contorted beyond any
    smoothing out.
The boy's long jawbone, soon to be man, juts up white, petalled
    with splinters, a floret of bone.
If only they are dead, not dying. . . .
She whispers their names.
She is wearied with pacing to the window, cannot stop pacing
    to the window.
She calls to them loudly.
She summons love,
She squeezes and compresses it into her strongest love,
She magnetises love to draw them home.

The window is empty.

She tries to rest,
Hammocks herself on the sofa,
Stills her trembling legs and twitching arms,
Closes eyes, breathes slowly and with deliberation.

Behind the shield of calm,
Love is swinging and rushing.
Love is rocking and banging at her heart,
Love is making again a shelter of womb.
Love is jerking to the rhythm of union,
Love cannot bear the nothing of separation.
Love is leaping and running to find them,
Love is beating back flames,
Love is scrabbling in the ruins of earthquake,
Love is perjuring truth in a courtroom.

Love, raw love, is spurting hot from the breast.
Love cannot be still, love cannot bear waiting.
The children, the children are late.

MARGARET BELL

How She Feared for Him

Her son descended the powdered ocean
through the pierced planes
      of the half dense half green sea
his face washed well, which it never was
a lead two inch diver in his vast bath
head erect, knees, feet together
dropping like a lost policeman
freely, soberly and soundless
sacrificial and vertical
down to the water bottom.

She waved to her son falling
through the pierced planes of the sobersides sea
the smile on his apply cheek
split – split to a look of horror
through the green attic just below the surface
daylit, he sank through to the main
      mansion of the gulf.

She assumed he'd rise   three times
and come out
but he did not
      it was murder in the dark.

She saw him pass like a sliderule
      to the ocean cellar
her hands she found pasted palm to palm
so she couldn't dive even as a gesture
she wrenched her heart like an anemone
his stilled baby's blood on her hands –
his wrinkled and dwarfed look
intensely pleading his mother
      then shot of life.

Descending like a two inch lead diver
head erect, knees and feet together
like a lost policeman
going down to her crime.

JUDITH KAZANTZIS

The Custard Jug

Exiled to top shelf for lack of use
And taken down last week to wash,
It still contained the past.
How he had feasted on my custard!
'Out of this world!' he would state between mouthfuls.
Smooth, creamy, sweet, it smoothed, sweetened and creamed
His rebel roughness, until I thought
Its solace would hold him for all time,
Tied in my web of tenderness.
I was wrong. He found his way to freedom;
To travel untamed acres, and now
When I hear his voice across six thousand miles,
Warm but not aching; loving but not needing,
I know just where the mesh is wound.

BEATE LUX SMEED

Distance Vision

At the new moon of your birth I wished
For you a life without delusion.
Any mother for any daughter
Would do the same; a wish that reaches
Past the stars. I could not see
What light years from the real world it was,
And that I of all your universe
Would be the most deceptive.

PAMELA WILKIE

184

End of Childbearing

Oh skin of my skin
twice I netted you in
cast you out

I was womb-weaver
glittering with sperm

bodymaker eye colour
voice in the bloodstream

Two children I bore
male and female
perfect limbs
solid on ground

But two bodyshells
two summer planets
have cast their roundness
from me

have disappeared
behind the dark face
of the moon

who takes her pill
each night
without mistake

but rises
red and weeping
each month.

VALERIE SINASON

Grande Jetée

Some rhythms must remain unbroken.

like a dancer in an
arabesque
some women cannot carry
a child
in their arms

some come to salvation
drawn by the hands of small children

some can only make their leaps

alone.

MARY MACKEY

Fallow

I planted land that fell from the plough,
then left to dig my own furrow.
At the end of two harvests,
my own two children lie close,
warm and heavy as sheaves in my arms.
I huddle in to their sweetness.
In no time at all, a toy box is empty;
the farm set in pieces kicked into a corner.
Get back to me, love,
though the cottage is full,
I feel the press of an empty womb
and empty ground has the urgency of fallow.

SUSAN TAYLOR

Gestation

My womb has swollen three times, bursting out of my body,
And three times she has shrunk back again,
Pushing babies out into the world, to live with
The primal snub, of which each future hurt is but an echo.

My daughters are young still, with untried wombs and vast
    potential;
My mother is old, and has cast hers away, washed out in blood.
I stand in the centre and will not be pushed aside.
This time I will be fertile for myself.

I have asked my womb to take my soul
To lead her into the soft black warmth and lay her down
Brushing her forehead every now and then with blood.
And when she wishes to emerge again, let her come out, young
    or old
From her own private underworld.

MAUREEN RITCHIE

Persephone

That particular morning
woke me with a plucking
at the wrist, the particles
of the day gathered

Like an instrument, the sun
hummed through the clouds as I
took the air's chords
in both hands.

My mother always said of me
She's a clever girl – that
Persephone, that fruit
of my womb's making.

Something has dismembered me
from that tender praise,
my own dexterity has left
me clumsily remembering

The sinister fall of the day,
the sun filtered through the leaves
onto mottled ground where
I stood suspended in

The quiver of a new shadow;
spotted like an edible thing
by a passer-by who keeps me
under wraps in his kingdom.

To educate me in regret,
to feed myself on stony pips
of consolation – an employee of his
spied me out, red-mouthed at it.

I spattered purple in his face,
invented a spiteful owl who
follows me about. We are
screeching creatures both

of us turned inside out.
With every step we leave ourselves.
By my hand the fruit is split, at my
approach, the season divided.

What damned touch made me
undertake this tightrope
between the body and its home.
Walking upright, underground

what gap of memory do I leave
when I am gone
into that manufacturing
dark ring again?

When my pomegranate head
emerges on stalked neck from silent ground
will I be quartered to be devoured or
in my season left intact as stone.

KAREN WHITESON

Demeter Keeps Going
(for my mother)

This wood is Demeter's golden house
the sun slaps wet paint on, and
here the goddess tramps about, busy beneath
her skylight of chestnut leaves
yellow and luminous as glass.

She whistles loudly enough
to shake the trees, smiles at the soft
crash and rattle of nuts
into her lap, inserts her fingernail
to split and prise off the spiky husks.

She sorts and inspects her glossy
harvest, the kernels' truth. She
tests each seed with her teeth: sweet
or bitter, the taste of rain or rot
the smell of sap or the sour kiss of decay.

She regrets the spoilt fruit, but
labours doggedly on, stocking the hollow
bellies of oaks. Then, larders full
she packs down leaf mould, rotten
nuts in a compost dance: death is no waste.

She chooses the best of the season's goods
to plant, then squats on the moist
black earth and puts her ear
to the chestnut's bark. She listens for messages
issuing up from the roots, the invisible girl.

Demeter sleeps in her house of twigs
curled under frosty quilts. She dreams
that the coldness will pass, that the barren
fields will stiffen with corn.
She prays that her buried daughter may rise.

She waits for Persephone to return.

MICHÈLE ROBERTS

Praise Song for my Mother

You were
water to me
deep and bold and fathoming
You were moon's eye to me
pull and grained and mantling
You were
sunrise to me
rise and warm and streaming

You were the fishes red gill to me
the flame tree's spread to me
the crab's leg/the fried plaintain smell
                    replenishing replenishing

Go to your wide futures, you said

GRACE NICHOLS

Separations

All day the separate lakes
of our bodies lap their shores
in secrecy, and when we lie

down to sleep they spill
into the river of dreams
where soul and body meet

and when we pray, hand
meeting hand, the one
that reached up

against the one that hourly
rooted into the soil
of the lilybed. You can see it

in the children's eyes the moment
they first awaken, and the way
their hands go out in a slight

motion toward what was there.
Then they rise and stand
beside us. Our hands touch

but our lakes, all luminous and blue,
are separate, and the vast
fields lie between us.

JEAN JANZEN

Initiation

You know you have gone
outside the parameters which
the metalled roads mark
and there are no milestones
for the weeping heart.

The weeping heart is held
under the leaves of time
by angels with winged eyes,
that are never closed to
your deep passage.

Your deep passage is between
the thighs of the Mother,
back into the sigilled runes of
remembrance where all is the
dark before new dawn.

The dark before new dawn
is the eye before seeing,
the larynx waiting for the
first inrush of air to usher
the first utterance.

The first utterance is a word
that comes out of the future,
spiralling inwards from the furthest
peripherous stars, informing the
world you are about to create:

and the world you are about to create
requires that you die into it
through me . . .

My voice is gentle, child,
and my touch on your brow
steadies the flame.

JEHANNE MEHTA

A Little Lifeboat

I held you in the still lake
of my womb,
a tadpole's eye
floating in the gloom.

I fed you in the river
of my blood,
a gasping fish
carried on the flood.

You struggled in the torrent
of my screams,
a little lifeboat
on a wave of dreams.

Now I watch you from the island
of my heart,
sailing away,
making your own start.

JENNIFER SINCLAIR ROBERTS

Pain for a Daughter

Blind with love, my daughter
has cried nightly for horses,
those long-necked marchers and churners
that she has mastered, any and all,
reining them in like a circus hand –
the excitable muscles and the ripe neck;
tending this summer, a pony and a foal.
She who is too squeamish to pull
a thorn from the dog's paw,
watched her pony blossom with distemper,
the underside of the jaw swelling
like an enormous grape.
Gritting her teeth with love,
she drained the boil and scoured it
with hydrogen peroxide until pus
ran like milk on the barn floor.

Blind with loss all winter,
in dungarees, a ski jacket and a hard hat,
she visits the neighbours' stable,
our acreage not zoned for barns;
they who own the flaming horses
and the swan-whipped thoroughbred
that she tugs at and cajoles,
thinking it will burn like a furnace
under her small-hipped English seat.

Blind with pain she limps home.
The thoroughbred has stood on her foot.
He rested there like a building.
He grew into her foot until they were one.
The marks of the horseshoe printed
into her flesh, the tips of her toes
ripped off like pieces of leather,
three toenails swirled like shells
and left to float in blood in her riding boot.

Blind with fear, she sits on the toilet,
her foot balanced over the washbasin,
her father, hydrogen peroxide in hand,
performing the rites of the cleansing.
She bites on a towel, sucked in breath,
sucked in and arched aginst the pain,
her eyes glancing off me where
I stand at the door, eyes locked
on the ceiling, eyes of a stranger,
and then she cries . . .
Oh my God, help me!
Where a child would have cried *Mama!*
Where a child would have believed *Mama!*
she bit the towel and called on God
and I saw her life stretch out . . .
I saw her torn in childbirth,
and I saw her, at that moment,
in her own death and I knew that she
knew.

ANNE SEXTON

Journey's End

How hard we try to reach death safely,
luggage intact, each child accounted for,
the wounds of passage quickly bandaged up.
We treat the years like stops along the way
of a long flight from the catastrophe
we move to, thinking: home free all at last.
Wave, wave your hanky towards journey's end;
avert your eyes from windows grimed with twilight
where landscapes rush by, terrible and lovely.

LINDA PASTAN

The Miracle

First is the separation from God.
A journey through light-years.
Then the splitting open.

There are three doorways you must enter.
It is pain, beloved,
you must tear yourself into pieces
to come here.

The doorway of earth is in my belly
a spiral of cells
wildly threading themselves into patterns
blood and bone and nerve-ending
hands and feet and eyes
brain and tissue and at the centre
seed forever into the future.
It is quicksand, beloved.
You will begin at once to lose yourself
as you touch it
and it craws you under.

A spiral of light
is the doorway of my love
radiance that remains
sun in the centre of your chest.
But earth-time cools it
to a molten element
and earth-time sets it
to a window of glass
and the first pain shatters it
to a language of joinings
difficult as hieroglyphics

and still the pains storm it as it shrinks
inward tight as a ballbearing
till it passes through its own dark centre
and springs outward
where a turbulence of griefs
swarm and shriek in the dark
clamour to be born.

The great doorway is in my skull
the original I.
Spine is the waterfall, the fountain
that feeds it.
It unfolds, petal by luminous petal
like a waterlily. It has taught me
that growth is not linear, but a slow
unfolding of what was there from the beginning.

You must split yourself into fragments
to come here, beloved
because of the three doorways.
And so you know the pain of being human
before the first pulse of life
signals your entering.

Your soul will seek to return
to climb the umbilical of light
and mind, its shadow, will stalk it forever
darken, and transform, and deceive.

Your heart will seek to make itself whole again
in the love of a mate, who will be
forever too young.

Your body will find an exit, brief as moth-life
in its own sweetness
when the prison of self dissolves
in making love.

Knowing this, yet I give you earth, beloved
give you myself as an open doorway
open myself to receive your entering with joy
receive you with joy and not a shrinking.

Where the doorways swung open
I gazed directly
into the radiance you came from
and they have not swung
back on their hinges. They are open still,
the miracle has been performed
beloved, you have given me myself.

JENI COUZYN

Change

Change
Said the sun to the moon,
You cannot stay

Change
Says moon to the waters,
All is flowing.

Change
Says the field to the grass,
Seed-time and harvest,
Chaff and grain.

You must change,
Said the worm to the bud,
Though not to a rose,

Petals fade
That wings may rise
Borne on the wind.

You are changing,
Said death to the maiden, your wan face
To memory, to beauty.

Are you ready to change?
Says thought to the heart, to let pass
All your life long

For the unknown, the unborn
In the alchemy
Of the world's dream?

You will change,
Say the stars to the sun,
Says night to the stars.

KATHLEEN RAINE

Notes on Contributors

Moira Andrew is a freelance writer and poet-in-schools, living in Cardiff. She writes mainly for children. Her most recent books are *Light the Blue Touch Paper* (Iron Press, 1986) and *Language in Colour* (Belair Publications, 1989) for teachers. **Jenifer Armitage** lives in London with her partner and daughter. Primarily an actress, she is returning to acting after a ten-year break. She also writes plays. **Carolyn Askar** lives in Elstree, is married and has three children. She is a drama and poetry lecturer and actress, and performs with the Angels of Fire collective. Publications include *Spirit of Fire* (Element), *A Unique Curve* (Priapus) and *Interpreting the Tree*, (Diamond Press, forthcoming). **Astra** was born in Manhattan and lives in London, she has two sons. She has contributed to major women's anthologies and has three collections, most recently *Back You Come, Mother Dear* (Virago, 1986). **Margaret Atwood** is an eminent Canadian novelist, critic and poet. She has many poetry collections, including *Selected Poems II* (OUP, 1986) and has edited *The Oxford Book of Canadian Verse*. She also writes children's books. She has a young daughter. **Sharon Barba** was born in Ohio and has taught women's literature. She is a member of Women's Liberation and a women's poetry collective. She is widely published in magazines and co-edited the *Rising Tides* anthology, (Pocket Books, 1973). **Margaret Bell** lives and works in South Manchester as a part-time university and college lecturer. She is a single parent and has two children. She has been writing poetry for ten years. **Elizabeth Bex** is of Anglo/East European parentage. She has two daughters and has worked in the Sudan for UNHRC as a refugee counsellor. She now lives in Sussex and works with families and children. **Sara Berkeley** was born in Dublin and is widely published in Irish magazines. She has contributed translations from Gaelic to *The Bright Wave* (Raven). Her first collection is *Penn* (Raven Arts, 1986). **Zanna Beswick** has worked as a TV drama editor, and is now writing a PhD/book on early women dramatists. She has published in magazines and has a published pamphlet *And For the Footsteps*. She also writes novels. **Joan Board** is an English teacher and lecturer. She is published in many magazines and has two collections *Candles* and *A Country Christmas*. **Eaven Boland** lives in Dublin and is a member of the Irish Academy of Letters. She is married with two daughters. She is widely published and has five collections of poetry including *Selected Poems* (Carcanet, 1989). **Judith Bollinger** was born in South Carolina and has worked as a tutor and day-care school director. She has published in magazines and her book *Waterchild* (Wildwood, 1981) is about pregnancy and the birth of her child. **Anne Born** lives in Devon and is married with four children. She has four collections of poetry (more forthcoming) and is widely published in magazines and anthologies. She is also a regional historian and translator. **Pat Borthwick** lives near York and has studied art, music and ceramics. She has won poetry competitions and is a member of York Workshop Poets and Pennine Poets. Her first collection is *Between Clouds and Caves* (Littlewood,

1988). **Sara Boyes** has worked in theatre as an actress and writer between 1966–80. Her poetry has appeared in several magazines and anthologies. She enjoys performing her work and her first full length collection is *Kite* (Stride, 1989). **Jean Binta Breeze** was born in Jamaica and is an outstanding performance poet. Her first publication is *Riddym Ravings* (Race Today Publications, 1989) and her poetry is also on record. **Angela Brown** is a creative writing tutor in Southampton. She is married to an industrial chaplain and has two sons. **Carole Bruce** is a mother of four, a psychosynthesis therapist and photographer. She has exhibited at the National Poetry Centre Gallery and has published in *The White Poem* (Five Seasons/Rivelin Grapheme) with Jay Ramsay, with whom she runs the workshop 'The Sacred Space of the Word'. **Rose Burnett** is an ex-journalist, now part-time tutor. She has published in numerous poetry magazines and in the women's press. She is mother of four sons and lives in Somerset. **Catherine Byron** was raised in Belfast. She studied medieval English and has worked as a reviewer and teacher of creative writing. She has two daughters. Her publications include *Settlements* (1985), *Samhain* (1988) and *Turas* (1989) (Taxus Press). **Katie Campbell** is a Canadian, living in London. She has recently published a poetry collection *Let Us Leave Them Believing* (Quarry/Aquila), short stories *What He Really Wants Is A Dog* (Methuen) and had plays performed by the RSC, on the BBC and Fringe. **Laura Chester** is American and has ten volumes of poetry as well as fiction and non-fiction; most recently *Free Rein* (Big Deck Press). She founded the small press The Figures and has edited *Rising Tides*, (Pocket Books, 1973) and other womens' anthologies. **Lucille Clifton** is an Afro-American and is married with six children. She has three poetry collections and other writings. Her most recent is *An Ordinary Woman* (Random House, 1974). **Mary Coghill** is a feminist, writer, worker in a women's bookshop, a Beguin (lay religious) and a member of the London Matriarchy Study Group. She has published in anthologies and is writing a book on matriarchal mysticism; **Angela Cooke** is a sculptor, art therapist and counsellor. She has had poems broadcast on Radio Merseyside and Radio 4 and published in various magazines. **Jeni Couzyn** was born in South Africa and lives in London with her daughter. She is widely published, performs and leads workshops. Her most recent collection is *Life by Drowning* (Bloodaxe, 1985) and she edited *The Bloodaxe Book of Contemporary Women Poets* (1985) and *Singing Down the Bones* (Women's Press, 1989). **Margaret Crane** is married with a son. She teaches English and has had four plays broadcast by the BBC. She also writes novels and has published poems in magazines. **Jill Dawson** is a poet and writer of short stories from Yorkshire now living in London with friends and her baby. She has published in numerous magazines and is editing a teenage collection for Women's Press. **Val Denton** is a part-time teacher and mother, living in South London. She has written poetry most of her life, finding it links inner and outer experiences. Her work stems from meditations, retreats and psychosynthesis and she likes to combine it with music and dance and move it off the page. **Krista Dickson** is a community artist, muralist and writer and lives in Kent.

She has previously published illustrated poetry and prose in the small press, plus extensive performance work and workshops. She has two children. **Ger Duffy** was born in Southern Ireland and now is currently Writer in Residence for Lewisham. Her play *Into the Night* (Sheffield University Press) won an award and was performed. Her poetry and short stories have appeared in numerous magazines and radio. **Helen Dunmore** lives in Bristol with her family. She won the Alice Hunt Bartlett Award and has three collections of poetry *The Apple Fall, Sea Skater* and *The Raw Gardens* (Bloodaxe, 1983, 1985, 1988). **Menna Elfyn** is a Welsh feminist poet, author of five volumes of poetry, translated into English and Catalan, and editor of anthologies of peace poems and contemporary Women's verse. She won the Arts Council prize at the 1977 Eisteddfod and has written a multi-lingual play. **Lauris Edmond** is a leading New Zealand poet. She has written several plays, published a novel and nine poetry collections. She won the Commonwealth Poetry Prize 1985 and recently published *Selected Poems* (Oxford University Press, 1985) and *Seasons and Creatures* (Bloodaxe Books, 1986). **Gloria Escoffery** is a well known Jamaican painter and her poems have appeared in many Caribbean literary magazines and the anthologies *Penguin Book of Caribbean Verse* (*1986*) and *From Our Yard* (Institute of Jamaica Publications). Her collection *Loggerheads* (Sandberry) launched a new series of Jamaican poets. **Christine Evans** lives with her family in North Wales and has published several collections of poetry, including *Looking Inland* and *Cometary Phases* (Seren Books, 1989). **Vicki Feaver** lives in Nottinghamshire. She read music at Durham and has published a volume of poetry *Close Relatives* (Secker and Warburg, 1981). **Jennie Fontana** lives in Brighton and has two children. She is a full-time writer and her work is widely published in the poetry press. She was runner-up in the World Wide Fund for Nature/*Guardian* Competition, 1989. **Janet Frame** is a New Zealand poet and writer who has been published in anthologies and journals and in the book *Pocket Minor* (Pegasus). **Katherine Gallagher** was born in Australia, now living in London. She has four poetry books: *The Eye's Circle* (Rigmarole, 1975), *Tributories of the Love-Song* (Angus and Robertson, 1978), *Passengers to the City* (Hale and Ironmonger, 1985) and *Fish Rings on Water* (Forest, 1989). **Pamela Gillilan** lives in Bath. She won a Cheltenham Festival Poetry Competition and her first collection *That Winter* (Bloodaxe, 1986) was nominated for the Commonwealth Poetry Prize as a best first-time published poet. **Evelyn Pascal Grundy** is a nurse, now teaching meditation and relaxation. Married for 25 years to a teacher in special education, their only child died at the age of 17, shortly after joining the Navy. **Caroline Halliday** is a white, older lesbian, involved in disability issues, as a mother, daughter and friend. Her writing is about taking risks, exploring taboos and painful truths. Her poems appear in numerous anthologies and her own collection *Some Truth, Some Change* (Onlywomen, 1983). **Sandra Hochman** is an American award winning poet who has given readings and published in many magazines. She has five poetry collections, including *Earthworks* (Secker and Warburg, 1972). **Barbara Howes** lives in Vermont, with her husband

and two sons. She has won numerous literary prizes and edited a journal and books on short stories. She has five collections of poetry, including *A Private Signal: Poems New and Selected* (Wesleyan University Press, 1977. **Sue Hubbard** lives in Islington and divides her time between her children, selling antiques and writing. She is a journalist and her poetry has been published widely in magazines. She has won literary prizes and is founder member of the Blue Nose Poets. **Louise Hudson** has lived in London, Manchester and Devon. Her work has been broadcast on radio and TV and published in magazines, as well as in *Four Ways* (Phoenix) and *Some People* (Turret). **Hermione Huxley** lives in West Sussex with her husband and two sons. She is an English teacher, now working supply. She has written poetry intermittently since 1962. **Biddy Jenkinson** lives in Dublin and has been published in *Coisceim* (1987) **Elizabeth Jennings** is a prominent and prolific British poet. She is an editor, reader and translator and has twenty collections, most recently *Celebration* and *Elegies* (Carcanet) and *Collected Poems 1953–1986* (Macmillan, 1986). **Judith Kazantsis** has published widely in magazines and anthologies and has several poetry collections including *Let's Pretend* (Virago). She reviews poetry, edits for *Pen* and leads workshops. She has two children and lives in London. **Lanny Kennish** was born in New York, and now lives in Gloucestershire. She is an English teacher (Steiner school) and bioremedial masseur. She has two poetry collections *The Brook Runs* and *The Bloom on the Stone* (Wynstones). **Lotte Kramer** was born in Germany and came to England in 1939 as a child refugee, now living in Peterborough with husband and son. She is a painter and has four poetry books, recently *The Shoemaker's Wife* (Hippopotomus, 1987). **Denise Levertov** was born in Essex, now living in USA with her husband and son. She is a lecturer, editor and prizewinning poet who has many books of poetry, including *Oblique Prayers, Breathing the Water* and *Selected Poems* (Bloodaxe, 1986, 1988, 1986). **Susannah Lash** lives in North Wales, bringing up her children. **Pippa Little** was born in East Africa, and now lives in London with husband and son. She teaches for the Open University and ILEA Special Needs and is writing a PhD on women's poetry. She has work in various anthologies. **Dorothy Livesay** is Canadian, a lecturer and social worker. She has written essays, edited poetry and has many collections including *Ice Age* and *The Woman I Am* (Porcépic, 1977). **Dinah Livingstone** is an award winning poet and performer. She has many collections, most recently *Saving Grace – New and selected poems* (Rivelin Grapheme) and *Keeping Heart – poems 1967–89* (Katabasis, 1989). She has three children and lives in Camden. **Georgina Lock** is an actress, director and writer (especially musical black comedy). She collaborates with artists to devise shows around painting and sculpture through actor's improvisations. She lives in London. **Liz Lochhead** is a painter, art teacher and actress, living in Glasgow. She performs sketches, musicals, songs, raps and monologues. She has published six plays and five volumes of poetry, recently *Collected Poems* (Polygon, 1984). **Mary Mackey** is professor of English at California State University. She writes novels and has four poetry books, including *Skin Deep* and *The Dear Dance of Eros* (Fjord). **Gerda Mayer** was born in Czechoslovakia and lives in London. Her poetry has appeared in various anthologies. She has several collections: *Monkey On The Analyst's Couch* (Ceolfrith, 1960, a Poetry Book Society Recommendation) and recently *A Heartache of Grass* (Peterloo, 1988). **Jehanne Mehta** is a singer, songwriter and poet, in the Troubadour tradition. She has several recordings, most recently *Let the Centre Hold* (Heart and Soul) and her first collection of poems *The Burning Word* (Diamond Press), is forthcoming. She lives in Stroud. **Sally Meyer** lives in Brighton with her husband and two young children. She teaches physically disabled children and is a trained counsellor. **Joan Michelson** is a lecturer at Wolverhampton Polytechnic and has a daughter. She is co-editor of *Coming Late to Motherhood* (Thorsons, 1974) and has poems and stories published in magazines in UK and USA. **Maggie Mountford** currently lives in Wells and has published her poems in *Writing Women, Other Poetry, SW Review* and *Prospice* and has a collection *Poems* (Maple Tree Press). She has two sons. **Kim Nam-Jo** studied Korean literature at Seoul University and now lectures. She has published four volumes of poetry, including *The Flag of Mind*. She won the Korea Free Literature Association Prize. **Grace Nichols** was born in Guyana and lives in England. She has been published in anthologies and her collections include *Fat Black Woman's Poems* and *Lazy Thoughts of a Lazy Woman* (Virago, 1984, 1989). She also writes novels and children's books. **Rosemary Norman** lives in London with her son and works as a librarian. She has written poetry for a long time and is a member of a women's writing group. Her poems have appeared in various magazines and anthologies. **Joyce Carol Oates** is a prolific novelist living in New York. She is also an editor and playwright and has eleven poetry books, most recently *The Invisible Woman: new and selected poems* (Ontario Review Press, 1982). **Rosemary Palmeira** is a social worker, student psychotherapist and member of a women writers' group. She has published two booklets *A Tuning of Flutes* and *Poems for Birth* as well as poems in magazines and anthologies. **Cate Parish** is from the USA, now resident in England. She works as a primary school teacher and has had poems published in various magazines. **Linda Rose Parkes** lives in West Germany and has published her poetry in various magazines: *Writing Women, Outposts, Orbis, Pennine Platform* and *Wayfarers*, and in *Arts Council Anthology 6*. **Linda Pasan** lives in Maryland with her husband and three children. She has won numerous awards and a fellowship. She has several poetry collections including *The Five Stages of Grief* (Norton, 1978), and *Selected Poems* (Murray, 1979). **Pascale Petit** was born in Paris and lives in London. She has published her poems in many anthologies and magazines. She is also an artist and sculptor and has exhibited nationwide, including 'Pandora's Box' and 'Art and Rainforests' exhibitions. **Marion Pitman** is living in Twickenham, selling secondhand books. She has had short stories published in several anthologies and poems in various magazines and in a collection *Lunch with Veronica* (Eating People, 1988). **Sylvia Plath** is a well-known poet, born in the USA, who died in 1963. She was married to Ted Hughes and had two children. She published four poetry collections as well as *Collected Poems* (Faber, 1981). She also

Notes on Contributors

wrote novels and children's stories. **Joan Van Poznak** was born in New York, worked there as a professional singer and spent her life as mother, surgeon's wife and community 'pillar' until moving to London. She writes poetry and articles and sings in the London Symphony Chorus. She has two daughters. **Kathleen Raine** is a leading English poet and Blake Scholar and edits the review *Temenos*. She has published many poetry collections, books, essays and articles and appeared in many anthologies. Her most recent books are *The Presence* and *Selected Poems* (Golgonooza, 1988, 1988). **Irina Ratushinskaya** was recently released from a USSR strict labour camp, after serving four years for her outspoken writings and human rights activities. She has written an autobiography and has two poetry collections in translation: *No, I'm Not Afraid* and *Pencil Letters* (Bloodaxe, 1986, 1988). **Elaine Randell** lives in Kent with her husband and three children. She is a social worker and art therapist and has published various collections including *Songs for the Sleepless* and *Beyond All Other* (Pig Press). **Anne Ridler** was born in Rugby and for many years was secretary to T. S. Eliot. She has many publications including *Nine Bright Shiners* (MacDonald) and recently, *New and Selected Poems* (Faber, 1988). She also writes verse plays. **Maureen Ritchie** lives in Kent with her husband and three children. She is a librarian, and has just completed a book (with Sarah Carter) on information sources for Women's Studies. **Jennifer Sinclair Roberts** is a part-time lecturer, writer and mother of two, living in London. She is currently working on a collection of short stories. **Michèle Roberts** has published four novels including *The Wild Girl*, and poetry, *The Mirror of the Mother* (Methuen, 1985, 1986), as well as feminist essays. She has appeared in numerous anthologies. She lives in London and frequently performs her work. **Muriel Rukeyser** is a prominent American poet, a translator from Swedish and member of the National Institute of Arts and Letters. A prolific writer, she has many volumes of poetry, including *Collected Poems* (McGraw Hill, 1978). **Carol Rumens** has two daughters and divides her time between London and Whitley Bay, where she is Northern Arts Literary Fellow. She is widely published, including short stories, plays and a novel. Her latest books of poetry are *The Greening of the Snow Bead* (Bloodaxe, 1988) and *From Berlin to Heaven* (Chatto. 1989). **Carole Satyamurti** has lived in Kent, USA and Uganda and now lives in London with her daughter. She teaches at North East London Polytechnic. She won the National Poetry Competititon and her first book is *Broken Moon* (OUP, 1987). **Lesley Saunders** has two chidren, for whom the poems in this collection were written. As well as poetry, she has published a variety of fiction and non-fiction and performs with The Bloody Poets. She is a single parent living in Slough and working in applied research. **Edith Scovell** lives in Oxford and is married with children and grandchildren. She has published numerous volumes of poetry, including *The Space Between* and *Collected Poems* (Carcanet, 1988). **Sally Servian** lives in North London with her husband and two young children. She is a homemaker and writer. She has published poems in various magazines and booklets. She also writes children's stories. **Anne Sexton** lived in Massachusetts and taught at Boston University; she died in 1974. She won many prizes and awards and published eight volumes of poetry including *Book of Folly, Death Notebooks* and *The Awful Rowing Towards God* (Houghton Mifflin). **Penelope Shuttle** has published novels as well as several poetry collections. Her most recent are *Lion From Rio* and *Adventures With my Horse* (OUP, 1989). She also co-authored *The Wise Wound* (Gollancz, 1978) with husband Peter Redgrove. They live in Falmouth with their daughter. **Valerie Sinason** is a child psychotherapist and poet. She is a member of the Poetry Society Council and is widely published, including the collection *Inkstains and Stilletoes* (Headland, 1987). She founded Prodigal Daughters and Poetry West Hampstead and edits Gallery magazine. **Beate Lux Smeed** came to Britain as a child refugee from Nazi persecution. Trained as a medical photographer, she now works for the blind. Some of her poems have been published in booklets and magazines. **Deirdre Armes Smith** has four children and eleven grandchildren. She is a teacher and has written and produced plays. She has had her poetry published in literary journals and broadcast on radio and has four booklets. **Catriona Stamp** lives in a co-operative community with her son. She has worked variously as a town planner, joiner, plasterer and screen printer. She also writes short stories, articles and poetry and is involved with mummer's plays. **Penny Sumner** is Australian and came to Britain to do a PhD at Oxford. She now lectures in English in Newcastle. She has a short crime story in *Reader, I Murdered Him* (The Women's Press, 1988). **Anna Swir** was a Polish poet and feminist who died in 1984. She published nine volumes of poetry and ten plays. Her work appears in English in *Fat Like the Sun* (The Women's Press, 1986). **Kay Syrad** has had poetry published in Writing Women. She teaches part-time and is currently writing a novel. She has two daughters and lives in Lewes, Sussex. **Susan Taylor** has lived in Devon for eight years, since the birth of her two sons. Her last published poetry collection was *Rose Rent* (Turret Books, 1989). A collection of motherhood poems *Landscape with Push-Chair* is, as yet unpublished. **Elizabeth Temple** is an Orcadian who has recently published *Four Poets for St Magnus* (Breckness Press), chosen as one of the seven most beautiful books of 1988. She is married and has three children and lives in Winchester when not in Orkney. **Judit Tóth** was born in Budapest, Hungary; her parents were killed in a concentration camp; she now lives in Paris with her family. She has edited poetry and published three volumes of verse and numerous verse translations. **Ruth Valentine** was born in Sussex, but lives and works in London. She has had poems and stories published in various magazines and anthologies. **Jenny Vuglar** was born in New Zealand and now lives in London, with a daughter. She is involved in a women writers' group and her work has been published in various magazines and anthologies. **Teodora Weber** was born in Denmark and has had a varied career including nightclub singing, EFL teaching, looking after Rebecca West and is an addicted traveller. She has published four books of poems, most recently *Quarrel with Aphrodite*. She has a daughter, son and eight cats. **Pat V. T. West** likes to over-write male texts. In her novel *I Am She Am I?* she reworks

Ulysses. As a writer, she aims to bring a little closer the day when women will be acceptable not in small doses but in entirety. **Karen Whiteson** was brought up in London and Southern Spain. She has had poems published and a play *Tales for Louis* (1989) broadcast on radio. She is working on another play and teaches creative writing. **Stella Whiting** left school at 15 and acquired a philosophy degree at Leeds at 39. She is now divorced, seriously disabled but still living alone and researching in logic. Poetry was a therapy in crises. **Pamela Wilkie** read English at Cambridge in the fifties, sharing supervisions with Sylvia Plath. She lived overseas for 25 years, working as a speech/language therapist with children. She has published in various magazines. **Nancy Willard** lives in New York State and has published various books including *Water Walker* (Knopf) and *A Visit to William Blake's Inn: Poems for Innocent and Experienced Travellers* (Methuen, 1982). She has also written a novel. **Helen Wolfert** lived in New York State and died in 1955. She was married, with two daughters and four grandchildren. She has published short stories, essays and three poetry collections, the last being *Landlady and Tenant* (Sheep Meadow Press). **Judith Wright** is a well-known Australian poet. She has written critical essays, short stories and non-fiction as well as twelve collections of poetry, including *Collected Poems* (Angus & Robertson, 1971). **Marg Yeo** has been variously employed as a secretary, antiquarian bookseller, clerk, computer operator, lecturer and tutor. She is a feminist and poet and has published in anthologies and the collection *Unnatural Acts* (Jezebel/Gynergy, 1987). **Yosano Akiko** is Japanese and died in 1942. She co-founded the New Poetry Society. She was a leading pacifist, feminist and socialist and wrote poetry, novels, essays, children's stories and fairy tales. She had eleven children. **Barbara Zanditon**, an American, has lived in London most of her adult life. She is a poet and lyricist. **Evan Zimroth** lectures in New York. She has won a poetry fellowship and been published in magazines. Her books are *Gisella Considers Her Future* (Ohio, 1978) and *Front Porch*. She is working on a book of women's holocaust poetry.